Never Give Up

An Autobiography

Rick Gambino

Intellect Publishing, LLC

RICK GAMBINO

Copyright © 2020 Rick Gambino

ISBN: 978-1-945190-87-2

FV-8HB

Cover Design by Sam Gambino

Visit the Authors web site:

www.NeverGiveUpBook.com

www.IntellectPublishing.com

Dedication

To my wife Gari and sons Rich, Brett, Josh, Adam and Luke, for all of their hard work and heartfelt sacrifices.

RICK GAMBINO

Prologue

I've been questioned all my life about how I achieved everything that I have accomplished. I assume people think the small successes I've attained were somehow handed to me, and supposed access to money and influence.

This could not be further from the truth.

I grew up in a lower-middle-class neighborhood, ditched school and got into trouble – like most boys my age. I enlisted in the Army, sang in many different groups, married, raised a family, opened (and closed) various restaurants, went through a religious conversion, faced bankruptcy and finally ended up where I am today: an "overnight success" that only took sixty-plus years to achieve.

Along the way, I have collected many stories, and these are what I am sharing with you. I was a little hesitant to do so, but with gentle nudging from family and friends, I relented.

The stories of my early years may surprise many who know me. Truth is, I was a smart-assed little kid who was constantly getting into trouble (getting away with some and getting caught at the rest). I finally came to realize that what I was doing during those early years wasn't just fun, but in some cases was also hurtful.

As you'll also see, I made it a point to take my life in a different direction, which finally brought me to be the person I am today. Throughout the course of my life, I have had dozens of close friends, including many from my childhood. It is said you can judge a man by his friendships. If so, I am truly blessed with a rich assortment of friends.

In this book, I've finally answered a persistent question that always comes up: "Are you related to THE Gambinos of New York?"

"You mean, Carlo Gambino and the mobsters?"

"Yes."

I've usually kidded about the answer. "No, I just help them bury people once in a while," or "Naw, I haven't killed anyone who lived to tell about it."

It deflects the question, and, after all, I enjoy making people laugh.

However, notice that I still haven't answered the question … yet.

Enjoy the book!

Contents

RICK GAMBINO

Never Give Up

An Autobiography

RICK GAMBINO

Where the Heck is Lincoln Park?
HINT: Next to Detroit, of course.

A Little Background...

What is now Lincoln Park was once the Potawatomi Nation, with streams and rivers, lakes of crystal-pure water, virgin forests, and abundant wildlife.

In 1701, Antoine de la Mothe Cadillac and his group traveled from the east across Canada in canoes to Lake St. Clair, then south to Detroit, where they established Fort Pontchartrain. Seven years later, Cadillac made land grants to French settlers.

In 1776, the Potawatomis deeded 4000 acres of land, which included parts of Wyandotte and Ecorse and all of Allen Park and Lincoln Park, to one man—Pierre St. Cosme. After his death, his family sold most of it.

Prior to the Civil War, German immigrants came; and of course, Italian and other immigrants came as well.

Neighborhoods were first laid in the area of Ecorse Township, that would later become Lincoln Park in 1906. It was incorporated as a village in 1921, and as a city in 1925.

Thanks to Henry Ford's "$5.00-a-day" wage, many workers bought property in Lincoln Park, and a second expansion came after World War II.

That is where I came in.

Lincoln Park, Michigan

Never Give Up

Part One

From Hoodlum to Teen "Doo-Wopper"

Grandmother Grazia and Grandfather Giuseppe Gambino

The Early Years

I'm told now that when I was growing up in Lincoln Park, Michigan, it was the number one city per capita of juvenile delinquents in the United States. Maybe it was. I don't know. I probably helped contribute to that statistic. I just knew it as home to me and my family. Edged just outside of Detroit, it was a sleepy lower to middle-class blue-collar community that I called home.

Because Ellis Island was backed up, my grandfather Giuseppe came to the United States through New Orleans, from Sicily, and ended up in Flatcreek, Alabama, near Birmingham. It was there my dad was born. Giuseppe became a coal miner, working his way up through the mines.

My Dad top left with brother and sisters

From Flatcreek, he moved to West Virginia, eventually settling in Ecorse, Michigan, a suburb of Detroit. He purchased a large tract of land, almost three city blocks. He wanted land, because land in Italy was scarce. He built a house, the house I knew growing up, which was about ten minutes away from where I lived. He planted all kinds of fruit trees – pear, apple and many others. He also grew grapes and vegetables.

The area, of course, was white, and the residents preferred it that way (this was the 1940s). When a black doctor bought some land in Lincoln Park, on the border of Ecorse, and built a house, the city annexed the property to Ecorse so the home would not be in the city of Lincoln Park. Quite racist to say the least

Grandfather's family on my father's side

My grandfather's name was Giuseppe Gambino, but in English it was Joseph. He was married to my grandmother, Grazia, which in English meant Grace. He was medium height and thin. My grandmother was very short and wide. My dad was Rocco John Gambino, one of six brothers and two sisters.

My mother was Edna James. Her father, my grandfather, was Jolly James. He had six daughters and two sons. Rumor has it that he was a distant relation to Jesse James. Could be. He never spoke about it. If it is true, my being related to Jesse James on my mother's side and Carlo Gambino on my father's side could explain my adolescent behaviors.

Jolly James was a bright and interesting guy. He held numerous patents for inventions, including one for turn signals on cars, a ratchet screwdriver, hay balers, cherry pickers and more. But the most incredible thing he did was build a house completely out of glass.

Grandfather Jolly James' Glass House

I mean, he used framing of some sort, but the roof and walls were all see-through glass. It was amazing to be inside of it – it felt as if you were outdoors. I guess he knew the true meaning of that saying "people living in glass houses should not throw stones." However, he later had to put a real roof on it, due to kids throwing rocks through the glass roof. I named one of my first ventures after him, which I detail later in this book.

Grandpa and Grandma James

By the way, all he received from Ford for the turn signals and his other inventions were bragging rights. Ford reaped the financial rewards. You can Google him and see the various patents he procured. He died at eighty-two years old, after being hit by a car while crossing the street to his glass house.

My parents were married in 1936, and I was born on April 28th, 1941, the middle son between two brothers, Joseph Paul

Gambino (the older one), and Mark Douglas Gambino, my younger brother. I was born Gilbert Richard Gambino, although from a very early age I was simply called Rich or Richard, which I preferred over Gilbert.

Shortly before I was born, my parents bought a fairly large house on Wilson Street and paid a total of $3,000 for it. The house had two

Rick as a baby

stories, plus a full basement, and a three-and-a-half-car garage. It was built on a lot that was big enough to build another house beside it.

Our house growing up

Instead, my family grew strawberries and we also had a peach tree there.

The Safety Pin

One of my earliest memories still sticks strongly in my mind. I was about three. Mom and Dad were in bed, and my friend and I were playing with little red plastic pill bottles (more like prescription bottles). We were playing doctor, acting as if we were drinking out of them. One of the bottles contained an open safety pin, and I swallowed it.

10

My parents watched us play. When I started screaming, they quickly called the doctor. In those days, the doctor still came by the house with a little black bag.

I felt as if I were near death – which I was. After a little finagling, he was able to remove the safety pin from my throat, and the crisis ended. Thank goodness for doctors who still made house calls.

We didn't have a car, and really didn't need one. Back then, almost everything was delivered. There were produce trucks, cleaner trucks, the

Me as a toddler

milkman, etc. Most everything we needed came down the street – including ice cream! Anything else we needed, we walked to get.

We were what I would call lower middle class, but I didn't know that, nor did I feel it. We had no television, and as I mentioned, no car most of my childhood. There were even people worse off than us.

Just 100 yards down the street was my friend Dave and his family. They had a very small house with several holes in the floor covered over with boards. On occasion, you could see mice and rats. They took baths in a galvanized tub about three feet in diameter. At least we had a bathtub, although we only took baths about once a week on Saturday. Dave's mother and my mother were very close friends.

Rick on right, Virginia and Paul

11

I remember an older man who would come around with a beat-up old horse. He would make nice, get you up on the horse,

put a cowboy hat and vest on you, and then take a picture. Then, he would come back later and try to sell it to our parents for a buck or two. Since I haven't found any pictures of me on this horse, I'm guessing my parents didn't buy one.

Tree Climbing & Games

As I grew a bit older, I loved climbing trees and getting on the roof of my house. My mother could hear me running across the roof and would yell

Mom, my brothers and me

for me to get down. I was up there quite often. I also loved to climb the large maple tree in the front of our house. I would go to the very top and could see my elementary school, called Raupp School. I'm glad that I survived my childhood because I didn't seem to have any fear back then. In fact, I still don't.

We didn't have much money, so we played games like Kick the Can in the middle of

Tree in front of our house

12

the street. All we needed was an empty can.

One of the kids would have to tag any of the others before they could run in and kick the can sitting there. They all would try to kick the can before they were tagged. Then the kid would have to chase after the can and set it back up. If another kid tagged him before he could kick the can, that tagged person had to be the bearer of the can.

The Gambino Boys

There were a lot of rules for that simple game.

Dave B. and I used to play soldiers between our houses. Our houses were maybe 600 or 700 feet apart. I would start at mine, he at his. We would move the metal soldiers closer toward each other, carefully measuring the distance and coming up with all kinds of rules. I don't remember who actually won those army fights, or even if it involved winning. It was just fun to play with the little "metal" army guys.

Mark, Rick and Paul

When I was outside playing, my mom would constantly be calling me. When she yelled "RICHARD!", I knew I better come running. Usually, it was because I had failed to do a chore or needed to go to the store.

Potters was our local store. It was quite small by today's standards. My mom was always sending me to Potters to get

Mark on left and Rick

something or other. I mostly looked forward to it, because I could take a handful of change (usually pennies) and buy a bag full of candy!

Christmas time was always special. Even though we were not wealthy, we would still get one present each. One year, I got a metal steam shovel (I don't think plastic was invented yet). I was so excited; I remember it to this day. I played with it for weeks.

I never went to a barbershop. We couldn't afford it. My dad would cut my hair with the squeeze-type of shears that would make your neck bleed. He would whitewall me. He had us sit outside on the back porch in one of those old wooden highchairs and clipped away. I ran away every time I thought he was going to cut my hair.

Rick's house in winter

My First Look

Dave B. and I also liked the same little girl from down the street; I don't remember her name. We were about seven years old. I think she liked me a little more. We were always vying for her attention, and we were always trying to get her to show us her "privates". One day, she and I were playing and she told me to come get under the porch of my house, an area we guys had already dug out just enough to slide under.

"Do you wanna see?" she asked.

"I guess so," I replied, not exactly sure what she meant.

She lifted up her dress, pulled down her underwear and there it was. I tried not to act surprised but, being from a household of brothers, I was shocked – and fascinated. I had never seen a naked female before. I guess I should have been honored because she didn't offer the same view to Dave. She smiled, pulled them back up and climbed from under the porch as if nothing had happened. And, of course, nothing did except my receiving my first "visual" lesson in female anatomy.

Antics Aplenty

When I was very young, I put a couple of belts together by connecting the buckles and tried shimmying up a telephone pole like I had seen a telephone repairman do down the street from my grandma's. I thought I was really something. Suddenly, one of the belt buckles broke and I slammed down backward onto the sidewalk, knocking myself out. Not sure how long I was out. Woke up and had a splitting headache. I didn't try that again. I always thought that hitting my head like that caused my "sometimes" memory problems. I still think it might have.

Sometimes, when my little friends gathered round, I would take a towel, wrap it around my neck and pull it tight as if to

choke myself. I had practiced it a number of times and could stiffen my neck so it would not get too tight, unbeknownst to my friends.

They would pull on both sides and I would cough

Paul, Rick and Mark

dramatically, bug my eyes out and look like I was going to faint. Then, I would raise my arms slowly, and start screaming. I would release the towel and start after them, zombie style. They always screamed and ran away.

Great fun. Mostly because they acted like they never caught on, although I do think they knew. They just liked the fun. I never asked them if they believed it or not.

The first girl I liked was Madeline K. She had a half-sister named Annette B. Although I had the hots (whatever those were) for Madeline, my first real kiss on the mouth – closed lips – was with Annette, her sister. It meant absolutely nothing to me at the time. But at least I got to kiss her.

What Color?

My grandfather Giuseppe was rumored to be part of what was then called the Purple Gang. I think it was tied to the Gambino crime family organization in some way. I'm not sure – after all, they were cousins and lived in the same town in

Sicily. Originally, they consisted of bootleggers and hijackers who operated out of the Detroit area during the 1930s and '40s.

There are numerous theories as to the origin of the name "Purple Gang". One explanation is that a member of the gang was a boxer who wore purple shorts during his bouts. Another explanation is that the name came from a conversation overheard between two shopkeepers:

Carlo Gambino resembles my grandfather's side of the family

"These boys are not like other children of their age, they're tainted, off color."

*"Yes," replied the other shopkeeper. "They're rotten, purple like the color of bad meat, they're a **Purple Gang**."*

Basically, they were the equivalent of the Cosa Nostra. They became famous for the St. Valentine's Day Massacre. I am not sure if my grandfather was a member or not. He never said anything about it. I did hear a rumor once that my grandpa and his compadres drank cat's blood to show their toughness. It might have been when he was in the Purple Gang. Still, it was only a rumor.

I do remember when Carlo Gambino, my grandfather's cousin from the New York mafia, died. My dad and all my uncles wore black bands on their upper arms, which is a tradition when a crime family guy dies. I still don't know if it was a joke or if they were being serious and respectful.

In any event, Cosmo Caruso came along and changed everything.

The New Church

My dad and family had converted from being Catholic to Protestant. What I heard was that Cosmo Caruso was walking down 12th street, preaching, and went up to my grandfather's house, who at that time was not a very religious man. My grandpa let him in, and eventually committed his life to Christ. He influenced his entire family and they all followed suit and converted to Protestantism. Not only that, but he and my uncles built a church right next to his house called the "Italian American Christian Church".

Italian American Christian Church

Cosmo stayed on and became the pastor, and my uncles all took roles in the church. Most of the services were in Italian, but there were some in English. My uncle Frank was associate pastor, uncle Joe was song leader, uncle Dominic was treasurer, and uncle Jasper and uncle Sam were somehow involved in an official way. My dad was kind of the Black Sheep of the family, with no official duties. Instead, he would sit next to the exit door.

My early memories of my grandfather pretty much revolved

Grandmother, Aunt Jenny and Grandfather

around his house and that church. Every Sunday, my dad would take my older brother and me and go to church. Afterward, he would take us to Grandma's house for her great homemade chicken soup. At times, I watched my grandpa holding a huge live chicken and then behead it in the basement. I watched it still run around the furnace until it died. It became the basis of the soup for that day. I could never duplicate that soup at home, although I tried.

I so looked forward to going to my grandparents'. I was able to see cousins, aunts and uncles, and play games like hide and seek, kickball and baseball. Also, we got to go to Aunt Tresa's house. She lived a couple of houses from Grandma's house. Several of the family

My Dad, Grandfather and his five brothers

members lived within one or two blocks, as well. Aunt Tresa had a black and white TV and we would watch Hopalong Cassidy, Roy Rogers and Gene Autry.

At these family get-togethers, they would eat tubatini pasta (a very small pasta about a sixteenth of an inch in diameter) in the soup made from the chicken my grandfather killed that same day. They loved to eat chicken skin. I wouldn't eat it on a dare. They would also stick chicken feet, cooked in the soup, in their mouths and pull the skin off between their teeth like a crab claw.

My mother, Dad's sisters and Gambino spouses

In the basement of my grandfather's house, we used to eat snails, also known as babbaluccis in Italian. They'd be marinated in homemade red sauce. We would use a toothpick to pick the snails in red sauce out of the shell, and nothing was better.

Rick and his cousin Carol

For breakfast, my grandfather ate a wonderful dish called "pane latte". It was homemade bread, coffee and sugar in a large ceramic dish — fourteen inches in diameter and three inches deep. We also ate spaghetti and soup out of those same bowls. I always overate until I couldn't walk straight.

They also made Italian sausage. The recipe was 40% pork butt, 60% beef roast, with garlic, fennel seed, salt and pepper and stuffed into pig intestines. "Ats-a-nice-a!"

They made their own wine by the gallons, too. Dago Red. I'm told it was a lot more potent than grocery store wine.

Some of Rick's Gambino Cousins

Fourth of July was a favorite holiday of the family. We would go to Grandpa's house and cook steaks outside on the grill, with their special sauce – mint, garlic and olive oil. My uncles tied long-stemmed mint leaves together to make a brush. They would also mix broken-up mint leaves, fresh garlic, olive oil, salt and pepper, to baste the steaks or chicken. It was fantastic.

Cousin Gracie and Rick

My cousins and I would climb on top of the garage and pick pears from the tree that hung over it, gorging ourselves. And the fresh watermelon? No one could grow better. Grandpa had almost a whole city block of property. Grandpa grew grapes, pears, green

21

apples, berries and more. We would eat steak, Italian sausage and go play games with the cousins. Fun times.

In the Basement

Once, a bunch of us kids went down to my grandfather's basement (where he killed the chickens). My little female cousins would then run around the furnace in circles and let me lift their dresses when they passed me. It seemed innocent enough at the time, and again, nothing happened. We thought it was funny. I have a different perspective now.

I loved my grandpa and grandmother. Grandpa would sit in his special chair in the living room on warm days, layered in flannel clothing and a flannel fedora and never complain about it.

Grandma was a fantastic cook and their house always smelled like food was cooking

Grandma

I heard Grandma would chase my dad and uncles around the house with a broom when they were being bad kids, if they ever talked back or did something she did not like. I couldn't picture her doing that. As I mentioned, she was short – 4'6" tall – and wide. Her hair was dark with shades of grey and went to the floor, but she always kept it in a bun.

Grandmother and Grandfather

She was always generous but quite poor. She would say "Hey, Reech" in broken English, waving her hand for me to come; and with a slight smile, she would ask me to hold out my hand. Then, she'd sneak me a pack of Juicy Fruit gum, like it was something secret and precious.

She eventually had colon cancer surgery and made it through fine.

However, several years later, when she was on the phone with Jenny, her daughter, she said, "I no feela too gooda." Then, she had a heart attack while on the phone and died. Right on the phone, talking to her daughter. After all was said and done, my dad and his brothers, when they were cleaning out after her death, found money stuffed in

Grandmother Grazia

the walls behind the bed. Secretly hidden. It was wrapped in rotten rubber bands and falling apart. The Great Depression really made an impression on her.

I don't ever remember seeing her without her apron on, and she died with it on, too. She felt that she was put on this earth to give and not receive. She was eighty-two when she died.

My mentally handicapped aunt Connie lived with my grandmother and was a big help with the cooking

Aunt Connie Gambino

and cleaning.

It seemed all of my uncles and aunts and the grandkids lived within a few blocks of my grandparents' house and church. That's why we always got together so often.

The Divorce

I was eight years old when Dad was driving us to Grandma's house to go to church. About halfway there, he pulled over to the side of the road, turned off the engine and faced us.

"Your mother and I are getting a divorce," he said, matter-of-factly. "I'm not coming back home with you boys."

We looked at each other but didn't know what to say.

"I'll be living at your grandma's," he continued, "and I'll be seeing you every week and picking you up for church."

I suppose this news was some sort of traumatic experience for me as a kid, but I really don't think it affected me like that. I was sad, sure. But Dad was always in our lives and I took it as just another event in my growing up. It did, however, have an effect on me later in life with my family.

My Father

As time went on, my younger brother Mark went to live with my dad at Grandma's, leaving Paul and me to live with my mom.

Dad took us to Grandma's every week after the divorce. I didn't care for church at all, but always looked forward to the chicken soup and my aunt's house for cowboys on TV.

Brother Mark

My New Family

A few years after he left my mother, my father married his new wife Beulah, *after* getting her pregnant with my half sister Serena. Beulah was a wonderful woman and suited my dad well – in that she catered to his every wish.

Dad and Beulah

He used to have a big bell next to his chair and when he wanted her for something (like bringing him food or a foot rub) he would ring it. She came right away. She looked like Edith in *All in the Family*. Very accommodating. By the way, Beulah had no middle name, and neither does Serena.

We found out Serena was born with autism, and that she

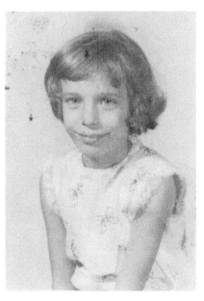

Serena

25

would need to be cared for the whole of her life. We loved her as our sister, and my dad made sure all her needs were taken care of.

Grandpa's Health

I was still quite young when, at one point, my grandpa got really sick. Turned out to be liver cancer. He went to two or three doctors, who each told him to go home. It was too far advanced to reverse – there was nothing they could do for him. He was bedridden and got down to eighty pounds, which verified his illness (he was 5'10" tall and original weight maybe 190 pounds). His face was sunken in and grandma couldn't even shave him.

Grandpa Giuseppe

Uncle Frank, assistant pastor, on left

I was a young boy when I saw him like that. If I hadn't seen him myself, maybe I would have had doubts about the rest of this story. The way he looked is still clear in my mind. It was very sad. He looked like any day at eighty pounds he would be going to meet God.

My uncles ran speaker wires from the church to his property, so he could hear the services held in the church every Wednesday and Sunday. What did we know? He was about to die. I believe it was the late 1940s.

The story goes that in the middle of the night, he awoke from a dream he had, with the strangest tale. He said in the dream he saw a light. And while sleeping he heard a voice.

"Do you want me to pray for you?" the voice asked.

He answered, "Yes."

The Miracle

The next morning, Grandpa started to get better. They say he ate a loaf of my grandma's hot bread. The doctors said it was a miracle. I believed it was, too, since two previous doctors said there was no hope. It was good to see him getting better. He started eating more, gained weight and finally recovered. He lived for more than thirty years after that and finally died of heart failure.

Country Medicine

My other grandfather, Jolly, used to take a small amount of formaldehyde every day; he said it was for his health.

Once, I got a serious infection on my arm, and no amount of antibiotics would fix it. The doctors could not stop the infection from getting worse and stated I might lose my arm. Finally, my grandfather pulled me aside, applied formaldehyde on the open sores and within a few days, it cleared up. Good thing, too. The next step for

Grandfather Jolly

the medical profession was to amputate my arm.

Stuck in the Middle

As I mentioned, I was one of three brothers. The middle kid. My older brother, Paul, was two-and-a-half years older than me and almost twice as big, at six foot one-and-a-half inches tall. I think he had a lot of pressure on him, because it seemed he was taking Father's role with me. He knocked me around a lot. If I had a chance to get away from him, I took it.

Brother Paul

However, one time when he cornered me, I punched him in the nose. What a mistake that turned out to be. I ran but couldn't get out the door quickly enough. He grabbed me and landed a solid punch right on my nose – blood everywhere.

Mom, brother Paul and Rick

I didn't get much support from my mother regarding Paul. For instance, she always said when I was sixteen, I could smoke in the house. I could hardly wait, although I started smoking much earlier. But this was permission to light up in the house. So, when turning that age, I took out a cigarette and lit it up. Paul did not like it and told me to put it out. I didn't. He

28

cornered me and told me I was never to smoke in the house again. When I protested to Mom, she didn't back me up.

I came to think of him as a total asshole.

The School Years

I remember my first day of kindergarten, my mom dressed me and walked me to school. I wasn't scared, just interested in where I was going. We walked the block or two and made it to the classroom.

I went to Raupp Elementary School – the school I could see when I was up the maple tree in my front yard. The tree was super tall and I could see over all the houses.

I didn't like school.

I was totally not interested. I didn't care where Puerto Rico was or what the square root for fifty would be. It was difficult for me. I am sure I had ADHD or something similar. I just couldn't make myself want to be there. It did not interest me, even though at times I tried to make it work.

Neighborhood gang of friends (Rick on lower right)

I think that is why I became known as the class clown – always making faces and goofing behind the teacher's back. I was known as the kid who was never going to amount to anything. One of my teachers, Mr. Robinson, finally moved my desk up to the front of the class next to his desk. Unknown to him, it made it easier to put on a show behind his back.

Rick in middle with clarinet

I got the reputation of being a troublemaker, a reputation I certainly earned. Going nowhere. My grades? Not good. E's were the worst you could get – there were no F's back then. I got a lot of E's.

The real reason I did not do well in school was because I loved to sing and knew from a very early age that singing was what I wanted to do. I loved music. While the teachers were running through their lessons, I was dreaming of my future in music.

When we sometimes skipped school, we would go to my house and watch Soupy Sales. My mother worked, so we had the run of the place. We'd sometimes drink a bit of her whiskey and refill it with water to get it back to the right level. This was in grade school. My mother was hard of hearing and we would swear in front of her as she couldn't exactly hear us.

Mrs. Phillips was one of my teachers in grade school. She went to the bathroom once and I hid in one of the coat closets in the front of the classroom. When she returned, she asked the class where I was. No one squealed. She then went to the front of the classroom and opened the doors to the coat closet to find me. "GET OUT!" she screamed. She pulled out a ruler and smacked me. She also gave me a one-day suspension, which only gave me a much-desired day off.

Suspensions were vacations as far as I was concerned.

Raupp elementary school

One of my classes was on the second floor of the school. Once, my teacher left for something and I climbed out the second-floor window onto the flat roof and took off home. The truant officers did not find me that day. But they did catch me every once in a while. Their job was to find kids, bring them back to school and then let the parents know.

There was this fat eighth-grade teacher named Earl Ball. When he got mad at you, he would throw erasers, chalk or anything he could at you. Mostly at me and Jim V. Once, Jim and I were put in the front of the classroom in order for him to keep an eye on us, so to speak. We were both always watched.

We had wood-top desks in the classroom. Jim and I decided to carve initials in them. Jim carved his initials, but I decided to carve my cousin's name on the top. Jim got caught and was in deep trouble. Mr. Ball confronted me, accusing me of doing it, too. I denied it. It wasn't my name on the desktop – it was my cousin's name, Colleen. I don't even think she went to that school. What could he do? He always held that against me. He disliked me immensely, and I guess now I can understand why.

Near Death

Later, a serious incident almost killed him. Someone put a metal paper spindle on his seat – the kind with a point where you would stick papers through. The spindle was about five inches tall. They put it on his seat, and he sat his 300 pounds of fat on it. Almost killed him. They said if it was an inch either way, it would have.

I was a suspect, but they could never prove anything. It wasn't me. I would never do anything like that. I think they thought my cousin Louie might have been the culprit, although he never confessed anything to me. I don't think he would have done it either.

Let Him Go On

When I was supposed to graduate from eighth grade into high school, most of the teachers barely passed me. Earl Ball definitely was not going to pass me. In fact, he said to many people that if I were able to graduate into high school, he would quit teaching. He ended up being the only teacher who failed me. I guess the other teachers barely passed me because they didn't want to see me there the next year. I had to go to summer school in order to get the credit from his class. I never did quit.

In high school, I had a foreign teacher, Mr. Tiapala, who spoke broken English. He had no patience with me and pushed me quite hard. I really didn't fear him, so I made a show out of it by sparring with him one day in a slap fight. He wasn't very good at it, so it was just a few slaps and then it was over.

He lost.

I am sure I was suspended for that, too.

Pencil Incident

Another incident was much more serious. I had a substitute teacher in high school, and when I could, I would always sit at the back of the room. Once, I was talking and she yelled at me to stop, but I kept talking.

She walked to the back of the class and tapped me on the shoulder. I looked up and asked her to wait and let me finish my conversation (yet another opportunity to entertain that backfired). She didn't take that rebuff

Rick and Dave, Joyce, Jenni and Virginia

well, and her arm came down in a stabbing motion like a bayonet. I saw it coming and pulled my head back. She stabbed me between the eyes with a yellow wooden pencil. The lead broke off between my eyes and left a lifelong black dot there.

It's only been the last few years that I noticed it had finally faded away.

The Fire Alarm

A buddy of mine came up with a brilliant way to get out of school. He and I pulled the fire alarm. It worked. The alarm was on a corner by the school on a metal pole. You would open the small glass door and pull the lever. They should never have put something like that in front of me.

It was too tempting.

Immortalized in Art

A friend of mine reminded me of something that happened while we were in school.

He told me that when we were in high school, there was this girl he liked. He was talking to her and was just sitting there drawing a picture of her. I guess he had some artistic ability. After finishing the drawing, he looked closely at it and started laughing. "Rick," he said, "It looks just like you!"

I couldn't believe it. It *did* look like me.

"I didn't do a very good job on her, I guess," he said.

He showed the picture to the teacher, and he commented, "Man, that's great. That's a great picture." Thinking he drew it of me. And he put it up on the wall, posted it.

The only accomplishment I ever achieved in school was I scored pretty high with the ladies.

Later on, my friend said, "Some girl stole it off the wall."

Projectile Hurling

During the later school years, we would skip out of school and hang out at the A&W root beer stand and drive-in. Hamburgers and frosty-mug root beer floats. We also kept beer in the trunks of our cars, when we could get it (we were underage). Root beer and beer. A not-so-good combination.

Once we skipped school and drove out to King Road; at that time, just a dirt road in the country. Two girls in the back, my buddy and I in the front seat; I really can't remember who they were. We had some Thunderbird wine. We each had a bottle. I came up with an idea. I challenged the girl in the back to a chugging contest, to see who could drink the whole bottle down the fastest. I was a smart-ass and thought this would make me look more macho or something. Just a way of showing off.

She accepted the challenge, at least I thought she did, and we tipped the bottles up and we were off. I chugged my entire bottle down, and turned to see that she simply took a sip, put the bottle down and smiled.

Rick in his topcoat

We drove back to the A&W and pulled into the parking lot. I opened the door and threw up all over the ground. Someone drove me home, took me upstairs to my room and put me to bed. I had never been so sick in my life. I continued to throw up in my bed. I am not sure if my mom knew what happened, although she had to have seen the mess I left.

They say certain events in your life can change your future behavior. This was not one of them.

The Beer Order

I remember trying a new scam.

I called the local liquor store and ordered some beer to be delivered to the house. They did that in those days. Of course, I was underage, but I had a plan.

When they delivered it to my house, they said it was for my dad. My friend answered the door, turned in toward the house, and yelled, "Hey, Dad, the beer is here!" to which I replied, "Okay, the money is on the table. Just get it and pay for it."

The delivery guy said he really had to meet my dad to sign for it. My buddy said, "Well, he is in the shower and he usually takes pretty long showers, if you don't mind waiting."

The delivery guy finally said never mind, took the money and left. My plan worked.

Basement Parties

Basement parties were the place everyone went to meet and have fun. We would go to those parties whenever we could. They were usually at someone's house whose parents were not home. The set-up was usually in the basement, with a small 45 record player and low lights. The best songs were the slow dances, and I took advantage of them whenever I could. I also took

Bill, Gary and Rick's Doo-Wop Group

advantage of something else – taking one or two of the 45 records they had next to the record player.

Over the course of a few years, I had quite the record collection, until a friend of mine, Steve, talked me into selling them to him to fund my going to some event somewhere. Don't remember the event, and no more records. Now, Steve has a great collection of 45RPM records which also include the ones he and I stole.

On a more positive note, we didn't always do things that were overtly illegal. One of the more innocent things Mike and I, and possibly others, did was raid neighbors' gardens at night with saltshakers in our pockets.

We'd pick beautiful ripe tomatoes and eat them under the streetlights.

Go-Carts

Once I built a homemade go-cart. It had small wheels and I created a steering system with ropes where you could pull on one side and the cart would turn. We pushed each other around and we thought we were so cool.

I also remember putting an old car steering wheel on my bike. Everyone thought that was so neat, having a car steering wheel on a bike.

Hard as heck to steer, though.

Movie Caper

Jim V. and I went to a movie one day. As we were leaving the theater, we looked down and saw a wallet on the seat. We both lunged for it but he was closer and got it. It had obviously fallen out of someone's pocket. We went into an alley and opened it. Imagine our excitement when we found over $600 in it! There were some cards saying the guy was a pilot for TWA.

Six hundred dollars back in the 1950s was like $5,000 today. Joey took most of it and bought a new car, and still had money left over. I never asked him if he mailed the wallet back or not, but I am guessing he didn't.

Me, I would have split it. He obviously felt differently about that – and our friendship.

Grosse Ile

Grosse Ile is an island in the outskirts of Detroit where old-school, fairly well-to-do people lived. It's one of those old communities, like Fairhope historical district, where all of a sudden the property got more valuable.

This was on an island and it had a real fancy golf course. And it attracted people with money.

There was one guy who lived there (last name Rooney, Dan Rooney, or Mr. Rooney) and all of us teenagers always thought he was some sort of monster. We used to call him Igor, and that name spread all over. He used to scare kids when they came around his house, which looked haunted, and it became a big deal. All the kids used to go to Grosse Ile just to see this guy and get scared. And he wasn't friendly; he was like a mean dog.

His house looked scary, too. We considered it totally haunted. We used to go there and throw stuff at the house. He'd come out and scream at us. Like I said, he was scary, too.

Things Were Different

As a young kid, we all would walk everywhere we went. Not many people had cars. I was about eleven when we would walk the sidewalk and pick up cigarette butts off the curb. Smoking wasn't a terrible thing back then but really wasn't appropriate or even legal for an eleven-year-old. We sometimes would get an adult to buy us cigarettes. They were about twenty cents a pack then. We would go down to my basement and play poker for cigarettes.

Life was different back then. You could hitchhike without fear. Kids could be gone almost all day without real concern from the parents. The main thing you could get in trouble for would be not getting home for five o'clock dinner.

My mom worked every day but still was able to get dinner made. She cooked mostly blue-collar dinners, like meat loaf, mac and cheese, mashed potatoes, spaghetti, stew, pot roast and things like that. If we didn't eat everything on our plate, we sat

at the table until we did. It was hard to find places to hide the food we didn't like or eat.

But we managed.

Performing

I mentioned earlier why school was such a burden for me. It was because music seemed to be all that I could think about. Not just listening, but playing and singing. As a very young boy, I remember singing "O Holy Night" in church. It verified to

those that heard it that singing was what I wanted as a career, and it went over very well. I guess I was okay, and people seemed to like my singing voice.

Near the beginning of my career, I was a decent singer. After a few years, I worked hard to get better and hone my skills. We caroled a cappella at Christmas time, walking from house to house, singing all of the Christmas carols like "O Holy Night" and "Jingle Bells". I can still remember the snow lighting up the night. People would stand in front of their windows or come to

Fan club picture

their doors and listen.

This had a positive effect on me.

I decided to start my own singing group as soon as I could. After we'd practiced, we accepted all sorts of odd singing invitations whenever they showed up, and many of them were in people's homes and at parties.

I also developed a plan.

Jim, Rick and Clyde

My First Manager

Ed P., a musician friend who was older than me, said he would like to manage me when I was in my mid-teens. He was organized, and we started a fan club. We got members and followers, figuring that might help me get a record deal. We ended up with fans in Michigan and even a few in Ohio and Canada. We went to a printer, designed and ordered the business cards, and then handed them out every chance we got. Big plans.

Ed and Rick

The point was, I had started my future career and yet I was stuck in school, a place I despised and where I felt like I was wasting my time. I knew school was supposed to be good for you and give you skills that help you in life. But I knew what my career would be, and I knew that almost nothing of what I was learning (or not learning) in school would be of much value to me. I was wrong, of course, as I later learned, but that was how I felt at the time. Although not what people consider 'book learned,' I do have what I consider common sense and feel that it has helped me in my future businesses.

I continued to sing when I could, go to school and, of course, goof off.

Later on, my manager decided to take me to Philadelphia to try and get me on *American Bandstand*, the Dick Clark-hosted teenager show that was a hit across the country. After getting there, we found out you can't get on that

The Embers

show unless you have a record out AND it is doing well on the radio. I had no record at that time, so no hit on the radio. We left, a bit deflated.

One point about my manager. Although he did not acknowledge it, and he never actually told me, he was gay. Not

42

overtly, he wasn't feminine in any way, but an incident convinced me of the fact that his preference was boys.

He came over to my house, and my mom let him into my room while I was still asleep. He sat on my bed, put his hand on my leg and started moving it up. This woke me up. I turned over, pretended to yawn and brushed his hand away. No big deal to me. I simply wasn't interested. To each his own.

It wasn't the last time I would be confronted with that type of situation.

Thief...

When I wasn't on the roof or up a tree, I was more than likely doing something I wasn't supposed to, and for some reason, I never thought it was hurting anybody. It was simply for something to do. I was probably a bad influence on my friends, mainly Mike, Steve and a handful of others.

Karol Grocery store in Lincoln Park

Back in the day, there were lots of smaller, Mom-and-Pop-type liquor stores. I hid in the ceiling of one. I climbed up into it from the back room and waited until the store closed. It was a long time in a very closed space. I don't know how I even got up there. It was a spontaneous move. Hadn't planned it. After closing, I waited a while – did not want to wait too long or I would get in trouble not coming home in time.

I dropped down, grabbed some cigarettes and some beer, and hightailed it out of there. They didn't have alarm systems back then. Told my friends about it and showed them the cigarettes. They loved it. I think they thought I was one of the shrewdest crooks around. I did that trick a couple of more times, then stopped. I'm not sure, but I think I was about ten or eleven years old.

I came up with another entrepreneurial idea after that. I would go into Neisner's Department Store, steal a handful of pencils, and then stand out in front of the store and sell them. I told them it was for the Boy Scouts of America. Most of the time, the patrons gave me the money and didn't even take the pencils. It was a great business. Neisner's never caught on either.

For the life of me, I don't know why I did it, but I remember sticking a fifty-pound-rated bow and arrow down inside my pant leg and walking out of a store, stiff-legged. I didn't even want it. I did get away with it, but I'm unable to recollect what I even did with the darn thing.

Another time, I took a blue jacket off a mannequin in the store window.

I can't even remember all of the terrible things that I did in my adolescent days. I am certainly not proud of them, but if I am going to write a book about everything I've done, well, these stories need to be in it.

...and Entrepreneur

Lest you should think that all of my youthful activities were "hoodlum" in nature, I was also coming up with more traditional ways of using my creativity. One of my first "honest" entrepreneurial adventures involved my uncles loving to fish. They would catch dozens of large carp, a fish I had no interest in eating. They were huge. My uncles would give them to me and I would pull a wagon down the block across Outer Drive, over into an area about a block away that was officially on the border of Ecorse and Detroit. I would sell these fish for twenty-five cents to the black folks there.

I also started selling popsicles and Good Humor cream sticks in this same area from my bike. I put a Good Humor freezer-like box on it. However, that stopped when one day this little black boy bought one. I don't know how, but after licking it, the bar stuck to his lip. He started crying. I panicked and yanked it off him. His lip bled everywhere. I was scared his dad would come after me, so I got the heck out of there.

Although that was the end of those early entrepreneurial dreams, I did come up with more, later on, that influenced my future singing career and other entrepreneurial ventures.

I did get a couple of neat jobs as a youth.

One was a safety crossing guard. I wore a white belt with a white sash (like a safety belt is today) and would help kids cross the street when they were coming and going to school. I was one of many, because they would alternate kids to be safeties. It didn't last very long.

The other was a pin setter at a bowling alley.

Paper Route

I remember thinking that delivering papers was a great way to make a little money. I contacted the Detroit Free Press who gave me a route near my house.

They delivered the papers at about 4am, which was pretty early even for me. My mom and I would get up, drag the papers into the house and fold each one.

Then we'd pile them into bags on the handlebars of my bike and I would take off and deliver them. Problem was, I was a little guy. In the summer it was not so much a problem. However, when there was snow, I would have difficulty steering and literally fall over into the cold snow. Getting the bike up with the papers and the slush was difficult too.

After doing this a while I realized I was not cut out for delivering papers and decided to try my hands at other types of work.

Settin' Those Pins

I was hired to set up pins at Lincoln Park Bowling Alley,

Fort Park Bowling Alley

working in the pits. I would manually set up pins between sets. It wasn't hard work, but tedious. They didn't have automatic pin setting machines back then.

Working beside me on another lane was Tommy, known as Snuffy, a yellow-toothed, overweight and quite nasty-looking kid, whose mother was known as a prostitute. She was big, fat and ugly. She probably had to pay the men.

We had two jobs. One, to set up the bowling pins, and two, to pick up the ball and set it on the rails to roll back to the bowler.

One day, I smelled something … funny. I looked over and could see Snuffy working the pit next to me. He smelled all the time anyway, but this was new. The smell got more pronounced, and I recognized it. Shit.

Where is that coming from?

I went to the front of the bowling alley where the owner and some men stood, talking. I could see the owner was madder than heck.

"That asshole sent a ball down the return to a customer with shit on it," he said.

The other men were pissed, too. Turns out Snuffy pooped his pants, got it all over the floor inside the pit and kept right on working. The ball rolled in it and he didn't clean it off, sending it back.

Yuck.

Tommy also pooped in the pool at school. It was like in Caddy Shack, where they had to drain the entire pool and clean the sides.

The ironic part is this: Tommy was a really nice guy. Pleasant and friendly. He was dealt a really tough hand with his mother being a prostitute and with his living arrangements.

But you really have to wonder: What was going on in his mind?

The Car Wash Story

My friend Richard K. had a sister named Irene, who people referred to as being a little "mentally slow". She worked at the car wash we sometimes worked at (which was hard work, by the way). Chuck, the guy who owned that local car wash, was overweight and a pretty disgusting guy. He was rumored to be having an affair with Irene.

Turns out he was.

Not only that, but the last time they were engaged in carnal activities in the woods, he died right on top of her. He was so big, and she so slight, that she was unable to get him off of her, so she laid there screaming for help until it arrived. Made the papers and everything. Not sure how long they laid there.

Lot of gossip on that one.

The Gun

Like most kids my age, I was given a set of cowboy guns with holsters, and I suspect a cowboy hat as well. You could put those red caps into where the bullets were supposed to go, and when you pulled the trigger it would make a bang. It was basically a cap gun.

Actual reformatted gun

The bigger point is, I also had my mind churning about something else. *Could I make these into real guns?* I was maybe ten or eleven years old. I don't

48

know why I thought about this. But I did. After figuring it out, I went to work.

I found a copper tube that would work for .22 caliber shells, cut it down to the length of the gun, wrapped it in cloth electrical tape. The gun came apart in two halves. I placed the wrapped copper tube in it and wrapped wire around the barrel to keep the two halves together. I also filed a little piece to a point on the hammer in order for it to hit the center of the bullet.

But I had a problem. How to get the hammer to work correctly? I fixed it by wrapping a rubber band around a notch on the gun to a notch on the hammer, where I could pull the hammer back and it would snap shut.

I put a .22 bullet in it (I am not even sure where I got it from), aimed it at a target and let it go. BAM! A bullet shot out of it.

All from a regular cap gun.

I still have the gun. And, to this day, I am still not sure why I did it.

The Carnival Caper

There was a carnival in town, and we all went to it. It had a shooting gallery where a bunch of us stopped. When the carny's back was turned, I unscrewed the nut on the chain that was holding the gun and stole it. The guy came back to check and saw the rifle was gone. Mike and I quickly left but the other two guys stayed there at the gallery. The carny guy chased us around the corner.

I stuck the gun under something in the alley and I wasn't going to give it back to him. Then the police came and one of the cops wanted to beat the hell out of us. It was one good cop/one bad cop.

Mike said, "Rich, we're caught. You might as well give him the rifle and hope he doesn't press charges."

I did give it back, and they didn't press charges. I told them that the other guys weren't involved in it. I was the one who stole it. The others had nothing to do with it. Which wasn't true because Mike and I both took turns getting the nut off.

But I took the blame, knowing that it would not make my reputation any worse than it already was.

The Chain Gang

We had a little group we called the Chain Gang. We thought we were tough guys. I think my buddy Mike was a bad influence on me (just kidding!) We'd shoot out streetlights with BB guns, just for fun. We threw snowballs at the police cars and then ran like hell. Mike said we burned fences, but I don't remember that – that seems too destructive. But it is possible. And by the way, if I did remember everything, this book wouldn't fit in my car.

Mike told me that some fourteen-year-old girl was writing in chalk on the sidewalks and at the school, "Rich + whatever her name was". Like I was dating her, where everybody could see it. And everybody was asking me if I liked this girl. (I don't remember who it was.) It pissed me off at her and I called her out on it.

Mike, Mark and I had been drinking (we were only fourteen years old), and I was standing there arguing with her when a cop car pulled up.

We took off running because we'd been drinking. Mike got caught because he hid under a car and left his feet sticking out, but Mark and I got away. Mike had big, ugly feet. I knew they would get him in trouble someday. I don't remember what happened to the girl or our supposed love affair.

Long before I was old enough to legally drive, when I was twelve or thirteen, we would spend summer vacations from school just getting out of the house and goofing around. Everyone walked back then and threw their cigarette butts on the

Lincoln Park Band Shell

curb. We would look for the half-smoked butts and smoke them. I started smoking when I was eleven. I later quit at twenty-one when I got married.

We had no problem getting beer either. We would walk to Sam's Beer Store, about two miles away. Older guys would buy us beer there. They would buy us jumbos and GIQ's. (A big bottle of beer.)

Jack Knife

One of the games we played was jack knife. This is where you face off to each other with your feet together, and then throw a knife a little further out to the right or left, and then your opponent would step where the knife hit. You would keep stretching your feet until one of you got so spread out you would fall, unable to maintain your balance.

One time this old man, Mr. Sanders, who was a neighbor, walked by and told us to stop. We didn't. Mr. Sanders was mean, a real jerk, and nobody liked him. He picked up a brick and dropped it on Woody's brother's ankle. He screamed in pain. Later, Woody's dad stormed down the street and dealt with old man Sanders. His dad was so big you could feel the ground shake as he walked down the street.

Old man Sanders never bothered us again.

Hitchhiking

Back in the day, it was no big deal to hitchhike to get around – there was usually nothing to worry about.

Once, Mike and I were hitchhiking and a car pulled up on Southfield Avenue. I got in and Mike pushed me into the middle and grabbed shotgun.

The guy started asking us questions about ourselves. All of a sudden, he reached down and grabbed my genitals. I jumped and began to raise hell.

"Stop this car right now!" I shouted. "Let me out of here!" He screeched to a halt and we jumped out. As he pulled away, I kicked his car and put a dent in the side.

Rick in front of Dad's 1949 Ford

Served him right.

Snow Surfing

We also used to hop cars in the snow, when the snow was packed in the street. Back then, all the cars had bumpers. We would wait until a car came by, and it was driving slowly because it was slippery and kind of dark. We'd run from the curb and grab hold of the bumper and slide and ride; and most of the time they knew we were back there because we were laughing so hard. They'd usually stop, or we just let go and ran away.

Lincoln Park buddies

We'd also jump onto slow moving trains and do the same thing

Stolen Cars

In the early 1950s, I learned how to steal cars. Not bragging, nor even proud of it. It was more a rite of passage in Lincoln Park, and there was no one to tell us otherwise.

Someone suggested "let's steal a car." It was probably me. Okay, then how do we do it? We knew most of the tricks – some older guys showed us that we could take tin foil from a cigarette pack and connect it to two screws under the dash or behind the starter. The car would start. We just liked the challenge and the joy ride. We never planned on keeping the car.

Once I stole a car and the police were following me. It turned into a chase. I took a turn into a large parking lot, thinking there was a way out the other side. Came to the end. No way out. I whipped the car around and sped past them. They flipped on their lights, turned around and sped after me, their lights and sirens blasting. I turned right at the next street after exiting the lot and was going too fast to make the turn. I ran head on into a tree. It just about folded the headlights together. I opened the door and ran like hell.

I got away.

And then another time we stole a car. We took it for a joy ride. I was driving and I dropped Mike and Steve off first. As I was taking Mark home, the foil kept coming loose, causing the headlights to go on and off. The cops saw the lights blinking and observed me reaching under the dash to keep the foil from falling off. When they saw that, they pulled us over, told me to get out of the car and placed me under arrest for suspected car theft.

I was put in juvenile detention because I was 14. I don't remember what happened to Mark.

Almost Caught

One other time, I did that with Richard K. We were going to take a joy ride in this parked car. I hotwired it and started it up. It was a stick shift. After I put it in gear, the shift on the column would pop out. There was like a tooth missing in the transmission, and I couldn't get away. It kept popping out of gear. The guy who owned the car came running out of his house and grabbed Rich K. in the passenger seat. I got out on the street side and ran. There was a guy across the street, and he pointed at me and yelled, "Get him!"

I did a couple of Bo Jacksons on him and then ran around him and jumped a couple of fences. Then I saw the Good Humor truck. Everyone knew the Good Humor man and we rode with him in his truck a lot. I didn't tell him what I did, I just went around with him while he was dinging, about eight blocks, and then got off at my house.

Rich K. squealed on me. They got ways to make you talk, especially when you're a young teenager – they threaten your life. I ended up spending some time in the local jail until my mom came and got me out.

As an aside, during my whole adolescent life, I never thought about the consequences of my actions. Thank God, back then it was all misdemeanors and not felonies. I would have definitely been in the hoosegow for a while.

License Plates – and Cars, Oh My

There was a time when some older guys talked me into stealing all the paperwork and an inkpad with the official stamp logos, or whatever they were called, off the counter of the offices where you registered a car. I didn't really realize what the objective was; I was just too young and dumb to look beyond what they had asked me to do.

I got them the forms and the stamp, kind of like a notary stamp. I really didn't realize what I had, I just wanted to brag and show them I could do it, and thought of all the "atta boys" I would get. Later, after I got quite a bit older, I put two and two together and realized what I had done.

They also talked me into something else that was their main objective: stealing license plates from junked cars.

I would go to the junkyard – it seemed quiet, nobody else was there. I snuck onto the lot, took out my screwdriver and found my first license plate. As I was loosening the screws, I felt a tap on my shoulder and jumped, startled, as a surge of adrenaline shot through my body. I slowly turned to see Sergeant Dominic Roselle staring down at me.

"What are you doing, *Gambino*?" he asked, with an extra emphasis on my name. I was stunned.

"Nothin'," I replied. "I … I just like to collect old license plates."

"Really? So, you have a collection of these?"

"Yeah." I was starting to think I was getting away with this. Maybe he was believing me?

"And where is this collection?"

"At my house," I lied.

"Okay," he said, motioning with his hand. "Let's go see that collection."

Oh man, he got me. I couldn't take him home. I had no collection, and my mother was there. I had to admit it was a lie. I thought for a few moments. I came up with a whopper, although it was partially true.

"Look. I was working for this older guy. He said he'd pay me for old license plates. That's all. I was getting them for him."

"What guy?"

"I don't know. Some guy. He was an older guy in jeans and a white t-shirt."

"What color hair?"

"Ah, dark, I think."

"You think?" The sergeant grabbed me by the collar. "You need to come with me, Gambino."

He roughly dragged me to the patrol car and threw me in the back seat, slamming the door. I knew I was in for it. He'd collared me before and wasn't the nicest cop I'd ever known. I always felt he didn't like me. I hoped he believed me about the older fellow. I made the whole thing up, including the description. I sure wouldn't give up who I was really working for.

He called in the report to the station by radio and gave a description of this fictional guy and drove me in.

Lincoln Park Police

Jail Again

As we entered the police station, the policeman at the desk asked if I was the one. The sergeant said yeah.

"Hey, Gambino, nice to see you again. You're becoming a regular here," the booking officer said, with a silly grin on his face.

The sergeant took me to a room and pushed me into a chair. "You're in big trouble. You stickin' to that story?"

"It's the truth, sir," I told him.

"We'll see."

He left the room.

After about twenty minutes, he came in with another officer who looked at me suspiciously. "You ready?" he said to the sergeant.

"For what?" I replied.

He left and returned with a guy about twenty in a white t-shirt and jeans. He was really angry, pulling away from the officer's grasp on his arm.

"Is this the guy, Gambino?" the sergeant asked.

Lincoln Park Police Force - I'm sure they probably all knew my name

"Never saw him before," I said. And I hadn't. They must have picked him up further away from town. Most everyone back then wore a white t-shirt and jeans ala James Dean.

The guy lunged at me and grabbed me by the shirt. "You little punk. I'm gonna kick your ass!" he shouted. The officer got hold of him and pulled him away.

"I'll find you, ya little shit!" he screamed, as the officer pulled him out of the room and the door slammed shut.

Sergeant Roselle had a slight grin. "Guess we'll have to call your mother, eh, Gambino? She'll be glad to hear from us … again."

Dad Chimes In

I knew I was in deep trouble. She picked me up about an hour later, really mad. She said she was getting tired of picking me up at the police station. She also told me she had called my dad and told him about it. He told her he would be by later that evening.

My dad walked in the front door, madder than hell. He stared at me, and I knew it would be bad.

Pointing with his finger, he said, "This is getting old, son. Go out to the garage and get me a stick. Now!"

I flew out the door and searched the pile of wood. There was plenty to pick from. I tried to find the friendliest piece I could. When I returned with it, his face chiseled tighter, if that was even possible. He looked at it and said, "Go get another one. This one is not going to work."

I came back with a bigger one, and he seemed to be okay with it. He grabbed my hand and we went to my room.

"Pull your pants down and lean over the bed," he commanded.

I did as I was told.

"I'm tired of continually coming back here. You know what you did was wrong. You've been taught better than that." Then he added the proverbial, "This is going to hurt me more than it is going to hurt you."

Where has anybody heard that before? One thing I had learned a long time ago: it didn't hurt him much at all. I wanted to say, "If it hurts you more, then why even do this?" But I was smart. I didn't say it.

After the spanking, I was crying from the pain. He sat me on the edge of the bed. "When are you going to learn your lesson, son? You can't be in trouble all the time. You need to listen to your mother, you hear me?"

"Yes, Dad."

He left the room with me on the bed, pants around my ankles, my butt throbbing from the spanking. I really felt I had learned my lesson; at least at the time I did. I also think deep down I knew I wouldn't learn the lesson for a few more years. But I wanted the whipping to stop, so I was going to agree to anything.

Rick in one of his dressier moments

Later in life, I put two and two together and came up with what they were up to: the forms, stamps and license plates were being used to sell stolen cars. They would make the forms and license plates match. Thank goodness I was never involved with that.

I might also point out that when my dad did not come over to "teach me" about not screwing up, my mom would either ground me or chase me 'round the house, whupping my ass.

She was pretty tough. There was no such thing as child abuse or political correctness back then. Today it seems like children rule the household. Maybe a 'friendly' spanking on the butt might have a positive effect?

Fighting

A classmate of mine, Bill L., was the badass of Lincoln Park. He was one tough son-of-a-bitch. Bill would walk up to guys and knock them out with one punch. One time, he was talking to me while he did it. It was crazy, and I was glad he was my friend. I never was into fighting and didn't see the benefits. I was in a few, and only picked the ones I felt I could win. Remember, I was a small guy but felt confident if pushed into a fight.

The clan of Lincoln Parkers (which is sometimes what we called ourselves) would have events at Houton Lake and at a place called the Quarry. I remember a large fight between Lincoln Park and Flint, Michigan. It was terrible. One of our friends came back to where we were staying, and he was beat up pretty badly by the guys from Flint. We all took off to retaliate and the fight got crazy.

I saw one guy tip a baby out of a crib and use the slats of the crib as weapons. Everybody was drunk and fighting.

The place had a lot of cabins and I was in one of the cabins with a couple of friends. A guy came in from Flint, screaming frantically at me, with blood pouring down his face. I sidestepped him and threw him face-down on a cot and started to pummel him, and all he did was cover up.

So, I let up and backed into a floor heater. He stood up and came at me, wanting to kill. I quickly reached for a beer bottle on the heater, my reaction without even thinking, and struck him with it. He went down like a limp doll. That was not really in my nature, but I guess when confronted with someone who wants to kill you, you react.

That's what I did. React.

Oscar Performance

By then, the other guys had left and I ran out the door – into a carload of Flint guys, mad as heck. I was scared, but instincts took over. I ran up to them and said:

"Hey, those Lincoln Park guys are getting away."

"Where are they?" one of the guys in the car asked.

I pointed in some direction. "They went that way."

The bluff worked. I should have gotten an academy award for my performance. They raced off and I was safe, catching up with my friends and telling them about how stupid the Flint guys were. I still feel bad about hitting that guy with the bottle. I wish it would have been different. There was no news about anyone dying, so I felt good about that.

By the way, it made *The Detroit Free Press* the next day.

Speaking of fighting, I mentioned earlier my older brother Paul and I were constantly fighting. He was a lot bigger and older than I, and of course, he would always win. But one time I had had enough of his bullying and started swinging at him with all my might. I got a couple of good hits in before he worked me into a corner and pounded the crap out of me.

End of Our Big Screen TV

We were somewhat older when we got our first TV.

Once, my brother Paul and I were fighting near the seven-inch TV that had a sort of magnifying screen hooked over the top and hanging in front of it. First, he knocked me into it, and then I knocked him into it, and it fell on the ground and broke. It was full of some type of liquid. I think he made me clean it up.

Another time, my younger brother Mark and I were play fighting, and I pushed him through the front door, breaking the glass while going through it. It cut a gash in my lower arm while I was trying to pull him back through. The doctor said if the cut had been any deeper, I would have lost the use of my hand.

My brother Paul

My brother Paul and I had nothing in common, and as I mentioned earlier, I felt like he was trying to step into our father's shoes, so to speak, and create some discipline in the family.

As far as I was concerned, Dad provided more than enough of that, and I didn't care for Paul adding to it. I guess in the big picture I loved him as a brother, but there were also times I would have loved to whip him good. Pictures of us gave no hint at the animosity that festered between us, but Mom and Dad knew.

Paul became engaged to a girl I kind of dated earlier named Barbara. She was good looking and I thought they made a good couple, although my feelings for Paul hadn't changed.

I came to regret those feelings about him a lot after the accident.

Styling

I did go to hair-styling school while I was in my teens. But then I found out the association between male hairdressers and homosexuality ... and it bothered me. I got as far as finger waves and decided that this was not my best career choice.

Paul with fiancé

So, I gave them a finger wave and left hair-styling school.

No Real Girlfriends

For some reason, there were a lot of girls in my life as I reached the teen years, but none of them were really what I would call a girlfriend. I got along well with them, and they thought I was cute and funny, and believe me, funny goes a long way with girls. One girl, who later married a friend of mine, asked me to go steady. Of course, I said no. It ended up ion the Lincoln Park Railsplitter newspaper.

I remember taking one girl to a party (we all went as couples), which I guess was a date. We split up after a few minutes and I ended up taking off with some friends, forgetting all about her. To this day, I am not sure how she got home, and I am pretty sure we never had a second date.

I was selfish. As time went on, I realized that life wasn't just about me.

But it took a while.

Then There Was Gari

Gari's father was in construction and had a pickup truck. One day, she and a girlfriend were driving this pickup and going past Mickey's, a diner by my school where everyone hung out. I was crossing the street when she drove the truck to the stop sign, her window down. I walked up to the window and stood there. She turned and was startled to see me.

Gari and Rick

"Hi," I said. "What is your name?"

"Gari," she replied, and then introduced me to her girlfriend. We chit chatted a few seconds, and then she was off.

I heard through the grapevine that she liked me. She had just switched schools to Lincoln Park High, which was a few miles away. Truth was, she made a great impression on me. I was smitten.

We would see each other at different parties, and finally I asked her to go steady. Back then, you gave a girl a ring when you asked her to go steady, and I did not have one. But my friend John T. said he did and gave me one to give her. I think he got it out of a Cracker Jack box. After she said yes, I didn't call her for about four weeks. Typical me. As much as I liked her, I was so wrapped up in myself I even forgot about her.

Gari

As to going steady, although it sounds good and noble, I really did it to sort of tie her up by removing her from the available "dating" market. I was not ready to settle down, but I knew if I did it would be with Gari. She was beautiful, funny, and most of all, into me. We dated for a while until I decided to go into the service at seventeen years of age.

That didn't slow her down at all. In fact, she followed me in.

Rick, day before
going into the
service

Going away party

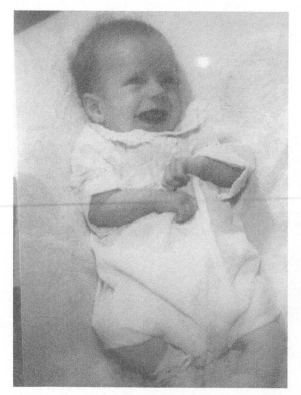

Rick at 2 years old

Rick with older
brother Paul

My Mothers family

Grandpa Gambino

Jolly James

Grandma Gambino

My dad and his brothers
on steps of Italian
American Christian
Church

Jolly James and
his youngest son
my Uncle Richard

Paul Gambino

Entire Gambino Family in front of Italian American Church with
Cosmo in the circle (Rick is bottom right)

Barbara, Paul's Fiancé

One of my handful of hangouts

Brother Mark
and Rick

Paul, Bill, Mark, Dave and Rick

Grandpa Jolly (in the middle left and in the tractor) and his patented Cherry Picker

One of my hangouts while skipping school, and the scene of where I threw up
the evidence of the wine-chugging contest I had to impress a girl

Paul with Barbara

My cousin Crystal. Shortly after this photo she was hit by a car and paralyzed the rest of her life. So sad.

Rick and brother Mark

Rick on a trike

Rick's sister Serena

Virginia in front of her
house and a 1955 Ford
Fairlane

Don't ask me how, but I did it

Paul, Mike, Virginia, Penny, Joyce. Steve, Rick, Mark and cousin

Pencil drawings by Rick

Danny Kaye

Johnny Mathis

Never Give Up

Part Two

Army Gives My "Potential" Career
a Time-Out

Rick is in the Army now

In the Army Now...

By the time I left the eleventh grade, I knew two things: One, I really didn't like school; and two, I needed to get out of it as quickly as possible – I couldn't imagine going into the twelfth grade.

My friend Tommy Good's younger brother Jerry was going to sign up in the Army, and we talked about it. We were young, it sounded good. We weren't at war with anyone, but that didn't really matter. It would be an adventure, and I was up for that.

Jerry and Rick going into the service together

Being seventeen years old put me on the bottom cusp of being able to sign up, but it worked. We both joined up together in what they called back then "boosting your draft." It was the same as being drafted, but we initiated it instead of the Army.

When I told my parents, they seemed relieved. I guess they realized I was not the ideal student they hoped I would be. My brothers didn't seem to care all that much one way or another.

One incident happened before I left for boot camp. We were horsing around in the front yard, and I fell down on the front cement steps and chipped my front tooth. I didn't have time (or the money) to fix it. You'll see what I mean when you see my pictures in the service.

When we showed up to process our way in, they split us up. I am not sure where Jerry went, but I was sent to Fort Leonard Wood in Missouri, and then Fort Riley, Kansas and finally Fort Carson in Colorado. First time really outside of Michigan. I was excited. By the way, when I got to Fort Riley Elvis had just left.

Rick in parents' house

Rick's company: 4th Platoon Infantry. Rick on bottom left

Boot camp was a real wake-up call. If you've seen any movies on it, they are all true. Getting up at 0 dark thirty, working out, marching; all the things I was not used to doing.

The funny thing was, I did pretty well at them. I was in pretty good shape before going in, about 120 pounds, and they demanded of me everything I had and more. I even made sharpshooter on the firing range.

When they issued boots to me, they gave me a size too small. We were doing a long marching drill. I told the sergeant the boots were cutting into my toes. He couldn't have cared less. He made me do the long march anyway. After a couple of weeks, my toenails turned

Rick in Basic training

black and fell off. I guess when that happened, they finally believed me.

I mailed the toenails home in a letter to my mom. She gave them back to me when I got out.

Later, I realized the ligaments on both big toes were severed and no longer could bend..

Bad News Travels … Slow

I was near the top of the recruits in boot camp after about five weeks in, when the sergeant came up to me.

"Hey, Gambino," the sergeant shouted, "The CO wants to see you, says it's important."

I knew there was nothing good that could come from being summoned by the commanding officer, so I braced myself like I used to in school whenever I was in trouble.

"Sit down, private," he said. I did.

"I have a telegram here stating that your brother has died."

I was in shock. "What?"

"That's all this says. I am going to grant you a one-week emergency leave to visit your home and help your family with the funeral. The Army will pay for the trip."

"Which brother?" I asked.

"It doesn't say," he said. "We'll get everything ready and clear you for leave."

I tried calling my mother but no answer. The only way for me to get there was by train or Greyhound bus, which was at least a twenty-hour ride. I chose the bus. The whole time there, I stared out the window, still not knowing which brother had died and

Friends, with Barbara in front

I didn't even know how. Plus, I wondered how my mom and dad were. *What's going to happen now?*

When I arrived in Lincoln Park, I found out it was Paul who died. He was on his way to see his girlfriend Barb (a girl I had dated a few times) with his friend Bob S. My brother was the passenger. Bob lost control of the car and it plunged into

Small Creek. Bob escaped but my brother was trapped when the wreck pushed his seat against the dashboard.

The coroner later said Paul died from the impact of the crash and did not drown. From the looks of the car after they pulled it from the river, I can almost believe it. I say "almost" because I still always said in my mind, *"Why didn't he dive in to get him out of the car?"* But I guess no one knows for sure what they'd do under those conditions.

Mom and Rick after Paul's death

My family was devastated. Especially my mom. I tried to console them as best I could, and before I knew it my week was up, but my mom wanted me to stay longer. I wanted to extend my stay another week, but the Army declined and told me to get back. I declined and stayed.

This turned out to be not so smart of a decision. When I failed to return, they listed me as AWOL – Absent Without Leave, which is a criminal offense. I was only seventeen years old and still had a habit of making bad decisions.

The Brig

I stayed and helped with the family for one more week, and then turned myself in at Fort Wayne in Detroit. They arrested me, handcuffed me, and two MPs accompanied me, handcuffed the entire time, on the train back to Fort Carson. I really turned a lot of heads when we made stops, handcuffed and being led around by two military police. They threw me in the brig upon my arrival.

To say they were pissed would be an understatement. They were never very friendly and now that I was in the brig, they notched it up.

****

By way of a little background, when I had signed up to join

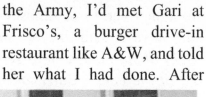

the Army, I'd met Gari at Frisco's, a burger drive-in restaurant like A&W, and told her what I had done. After

Gari in uniform

that, she decided to join me and signed up to be a WAVE in the US Navy. She was sent to Pensacola for basic training and then stationed there most of the time until they transferred her to San Diego.

Gari with friend

I called and told her about my brother, Paul, dying, and kept her in the loop of my AWOL situation. However, once I was in the brig, all communication between us ceased. She told me later she had no idea what happened and was very concerned about what had become of me.

****

Once in the brig, I became resentful and my attitude changed completely. I was extremely negative.

A few weeks after being incarcerated, they put me to work picking up tree branches following a heavy snow in Colorado Springs that broke them from the trees. We were to pick them up and throw them into a truck. After a few days of that, I didn't care anymore.

I started taking them out and throwing them back on the ground. Why? Because I thought the whole thing was absurd. My being AWOL and all. I had turned myself in. It wasn't like I was trying to ditch my military service. My brother had died, and I was helping my family. They didn't care … and neither did I. I was young and immature, and growing more bitter by the minute.

I found myself being thrown in what they called the box – what was referred to as solitary confinement. It was a four-by-seven area. A small sink with a toilet below it, and two-by-eights of wood to sleep on. And to be generous, they threw in two Army blankets. Nothing else inside, no one to talk to. They supplied two weeks of rationed food and two weeks of the normal crap they served. I didn't mind; I took it one day at a time. It was better than working on some BS cleaning job.

The odd thing I noticed was they wouldn't give me a fork to eat with. I guess because you could use it as a weapon or to kill yourself with. Yet, they'd let you shave with a razor. Go figure.

The Great Escape

A few weeks later, I was released from the box and put right back into the same job of picking up branches and other types of jobs, while two MPs with rifles kept us in check. When they weren't looking, I slipped behind a tree and waited. And waited. Nothing. They didn't know I was gone.

I hightailed it out of there and started running through the hills. It was not a well-thought-out plan. In fact, I had no plan. Just the desire to get out of there as best I could.

A few days later, I got to Denver and found a small grocery store. I swept and cleaned the store and slept in an old abandoned car outside that had a hood jammed in the front seat, and made a few dollars. I also found some old clothes to replace the Army clothes I had worn.

This lasted for about a month, and I decided that I had to turn myself back in. I could see I was going nowhere, and that I could not live like that for the rest of my life. I walked back to Fort Carson and turned myself in. This time, I went directly to the box and remained there for a long time. Seemed like months.

One day, I was brought before the CO and told I was getting discharged. He handed me my final papers, saying nothing. Turned out I was court-martialed with a summary court martial and general discharge under honorable conditions. Not even I considered myself honorable at the time.

The day I was to be released, the sergeant in the brig wasn't happy about it, and put me on a chair and shaved me almost bald. After that, they gave me my things and walked me to the gate.

I was free from the service. I didn't find out why until later. I caught a flight to Detroit via Chicago, where an interesting incident happened.

The Reunion

At the time of my release from the service (1959), O'Hare Airport in Chicago was considered the busiest airport in the world. And it seemed like it when I arrived. Thousands of people everywhere, rushing to catch their planes or meet their loved ones. I'm sure it would take a complete day to walk every corridor.

I was transferring to another plane to get home to Detroit, when I saw her walking in the opposite direction. I couldn't believe my eyes.

"Mom!"

She startled, almost in shock. "Richard?" she said. "Why are you here?"

I rushed to her and we hugged. "I got discharged. Why are *you* here?" I asked.

"I'm seeing your Aunt Mildred here."

"They released me from the service and I'm on my way home."

"Why didn't they tell me you were coming? I wouldn't have left. I'm here for a week." She was coming from Michigan to Chicago.

"That's okay," I said. "I got discharged under honorable conditions. Why, I'll never know."

"We wrote your chaplain when you were, ah, in the brig. Maybe it helped."

"Maybe," I replied. "Might be because I am still seventeen years old. After all, how many people get an honorable discharge after being AWOL?"

"Thank the Lord," she said.

"It's okay, Mom. I'll be home when you get back."

We hugged and kissed, and she took off down the aisle to catch her plane.

"Tell Aunt Mildred and Uncle Leo hello for me!" I shouted.

"Will do."

I caught my flight and made it home.

Home.

It seemed the death of my brother was the extenuating circumstance that finally swayed the CO to let me separate from military service. Not only that, but they gave it to me under honorable conditions.

Jackie, Rick, Gary, and John (guy who gave me the ring)

I couldn't believe it. AWOL twice and in the brig.

Maybe my life was turning around to a better place.

Brother Paul

I know I have given the impression that I hated my brother. That would be untrue. I hated the way he acted at times and resented his picking on and beating up on me. But there were times I didn't hate him at all. He was family, and nothing trumped that.

I miss him and all the things we were unable to share together in our lives since his death, and know he is waiting for us to join him.

But hopefully not too soon.

Gari with
Mother and
Mama Rae

Gari with
Mother and
Mama Rae in
hospital

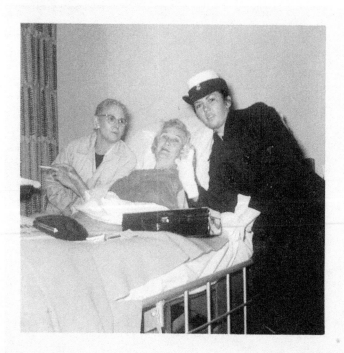

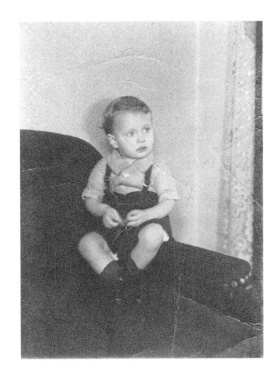

Paul as a baby

Paul in High School

Paul in front
of old Ford

Rick's Mom and
Paul

Barbara's Mother,
Rick and Barbara
(Paul's fiancé)

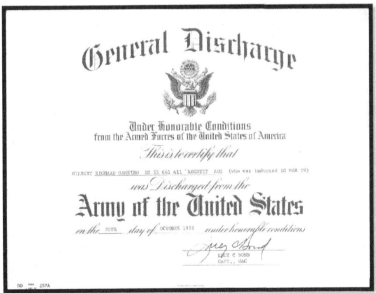

My 'general' discharge

Gari with friend

Gari looking bored

Never Give Up

Part Three

My First (and Only) Single

Rick Gambino

Playing Around ... Town

All of those hours inside the "box" in the military brig were used by me to think about how to launch my career as a singer (besides how to escape). I would visualize myself singing in front of crowds and it seemed almost real.

When I returned home, I reacquainted myself with friends, family and the town, but in the back of my mind I knew what I wanted to do – had to do.

Sing.

California Bound

I decided to go to California and take a break from everything. I had no car, so I did the next best thing: hitchhiked.

After I arrived in California from hitching from Lincoln Park, I found a local Arthur Murray Studio and got a job teaching dancing. I previously taught at an Arthur Murray Studio in Dearborn, Michigan.

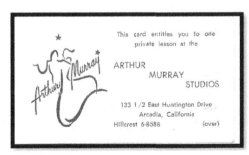

One of my 'dance' cards

One student who stands out to me was an older lady named Ann Russel. At the time, the idea was to sell lifetime memberships. I sold her one. And a very short time later, I quit teaching. That was not a plan, but it made my student, Ann, livid – she thought I would be there to continue teaching her to dance. I felt bad about that. It wasn't intentional.

It turned out students did get very attached to their teachers.

The First Record

I ran into a fellow named Steve B. He was nice enough. We were the same age and about the same size. He invited me to

Steve and Rick

stay with him and his family in a little guest house behind the main house in Alhambra, California. His mom, being Italian, used to cook greens and, of course, pasta. It was delicious and they were always trying to feed me more. Typical Italians. One day, Steve approached me.

"Hey, Rick," he said. "My Aunt Mary owns a record company."

"Really?" I answered. "What is the name?"

"Sutter Records," he said. "I heard you were a singer. If she likes you and your singing, maybe she can record you. Do you have any songs?"

Well, I didn't have any songs. But I told him I did. So, I sat on the bed and started to write my first song.

I had given it a name already: "What a Day That Would Be". But I was hung up on one small part of it, so I used *Oh, Oh* as a

Rick in Alhambra, CA

temporary fill in. But I never found an adequate line to replace *Oh, Oh* with. When I got to the studio to record the tune, I just left it in, and it stuck.

This was in 1959. The studio, located in Orange County, California, was fully equipped. The studio musicians came in and recorded the background music in tracks and

left. Very efficient, I thought. We also recorded another side to the 45 rpm, a song the owners wrote called "Love Me Just the Same". I loved the whole record-making process.

However, there was a problem getting my record on the air. A short overview will help you to understand the business at this time.

The record companies were heavily into pay to play – payola. What this meant was the disc jockeys

GOLD BAND MUSIC
PUBLISHERS AND PERSONAL MANAGEMENT

MARY DEAN
VICTORIA 9-5267

MARY D. SALERNO
CLINTON-7-0888-
5-6612

were demanding money to play records on the air. Big record companies paid as the cost of doing business, but Aunt Mary's record company would not pay. They'd already put up the money for the recording and pressing of the 45s. Hence, no radio time, no sales.

As a final note to the record, they added two female singers to the background vocals after I left, without my knowledge. I wasn't sure I liked it, but they owned me. I was afraid the vocals took away from the record. But the final reels were cast, and they sent me several cases of records that I sold locally. Such is the

My record, *Oh, Oh*

record business.

One last story about my trip to LA. I mentioned I was staying in a separate, small, garage-type building with twin beds. One night, Steve came in and I was trying to sleep. He sat on the edge of the bed and put his hand on my thigh. Sound familiar? I very casually pushed his hand away and rolled away from him. I guess he got the hint, because he never tried it again.

Steve would call me through the years, and I came to avoid picking up the phone because he always talked forever. Then, one day, I looked at the phone, saw it was him calling, and I thought "I'm gonna take it" and picked it up. It was the last time I spoke with him. He died shortly after that call.

Once I got back to Detroit (hitchhiking my way there), I continued the singing gigs.

Rare Rockin' Records

Years later, a fellow who owned a record company in San Francisco called Bob Pegg Records wanted my record. He was a collector. He found me through one of my past groups website and they gave him my number. He asked if he could buy a copy or two. He said the Rare Rockin' Records website price was one-hundred and fifty dollars a copy. I told him I only had three copies left. My kids might want one when I am gone.

CD that came decades later with my song on it

He had my record on MP3 but said he would like to own the original vinyl. I told him I wasn't interested in selling any of the three copies.

Some company must have bought the licensing rights to the record, because it ended up on a CD called *Dreamtime*, with singers such as Debbie Reynolds, Kenny Rankin and others. It really blew my mind that three decades later, after thinking my record went nowhere, that it was now doing well. I never received any royalties, but that's not important. It was finally a success. Especially in Europe.

You can listen to the record on my website.

The First Singing Gig

I was underage at the time of my first singing gig. I had a fake driver's license. They were made from heavy paper back then and if you were careful, you could change the birthdate. I

Rick and the 'reassembled' Tabs

was at the West Fort Tavern listening to Jack Rainwater and the Peppermints. I think he was American Indian. He was originally from Tennessee. Rainwater wasn't a strong singer; he was a band leader and he played guitar. That's the band that Jody Payne was in; later he became Willy Nelson's guitar player

Anyway, I sat in and sang the song by Adam Wade, "Take Good Care of Her," and they wanted to hire me as a vocalist. They were moving to another lounge in the same basic Detroit area called The Rose lounge. So that was when I first started getting a paycheck for singing; it was still Jack Rainwater and the Peppermints, but I was the main singer and Jody was the guitar player.

Jim, Gary and Rick

My dream of becoming a singer in a band was developing into reality.

After Jack's gig, I formed my own band and I just couldn't wait to drive down the street and see my name on the sign. It was over in Dearborn, so I drove there and saw the marquee:

"Rick Gambino and the Reasons"

Finally, my dream was coming true.

Dancing in the Studio

As I've mentioned, I got a job at the Arthur Murray dance studio in Arcadia, California. (I had already worked at one in Dearborn, Michigan). The reason was two-fold: for the money, and to enhance my singing career by dancing on the stage. I enjoyed the work and it has helped me throughout my career. I was very good at teaching it. I learned the steps before I taught them to others, but unfortunately, I have forgotten most of the dance patterns.

Reefer Giggling at the Diner

One of the dance instructors gave me a joint of marijuana. Later that evening, I met with Bill D. and we went to a diner to get something to eat. I told him about the joint, showed it to him and we decided to go into the bathroom and light it up to see what effect we would get from it. I should mention, up to this point I hadn't tried pot.

We went into the men's room, lit it up and smoked it. I guess we didn't realize how smoky it would be, because when we left the bathroom, smoke came out the

Rick looking cool

door with us, and we could smell it from where we were eating.

We sat back at the counter and waited. And waited. Nothing happened. Then I looked at this guy at the counter, eating. Ordinary looking guy, nothing special. But all of a sudden, he looked ... funny. I started giggling. Bill started giggling, too. Pretty soon we were laughing so hard we had to leave. We continued laughing, even after leaving the diner, and to tell the truth I felt pretty good.

I guess that pot must have been the giggling kind, because I don't remember ever laughing so hard before or since. I also never got hooked on the stuff, although I tried it intermittently all my life. I was more content with a bottle of beer.

A "Bump" in the Road

I saw Gari off and on over the next three years while she finished her three-year tour in the Navy. One time, she came home and we "got together" ... a nice way of saying we slept with each other. A few months later, she asked if we could meet. I picked her up in my car and we parked.

"Richard, I have something to tell you."

"What?"

"I'm pregnant."

I always liked her, but marriage was never on my mind. Now I was facing it fully head-on. I left and went home to think.

For one thing, I had my career as a singer before me. I reasoned she would be supportive of that, but the main pressing argument was the one I couldn't avoid: I got her pregnant and the right thing to do would be to marry her. Period. Although her mother thought differently. She didn't like Italians.

"My God, Gari," she said, "he looks like he has spaghetti coming out his ears."

In spite of that, I called Gari the next day and told her I'd do it.

I know she was pleased.

We went to the justice of the peace and had a civil ceremony. Fifteen dollars. When it came to the part where the justice asked if anyone had any objections to the marriage, I said I did and walked half-way out. There was no one else there. Gari laughed.

Gari after I said "I do"

We were married on January 22, 1963.

After Marriage

After Gari and I were married, we moved upstairs into my mother's house which had a one-bedroom apartment in it. We settled in and life was pretty good. I was playing gigs at night and making enough money to keep us going, while Gari worked on the apartment, making it into a home for our future family.

Rick Gambino and the Reasons was one of the highest-paid local groups in the Detroit area at that time.

Richard was born in 1963.

Tommy Good

As far as singers went, Tommy Good was one of my biggest competitors in Detroit. Detroit is a big city but there were probably five top singers. One of them, Mickey Denton, had a good following. There was also Jamie Cole and Gary Haynes, besides myself and Tommy.

There were many other good as well as not so good singers working in the area.

Tommy was a real good singer; he could really do it. He once sang with The Temptations backing him. We were good friends, kinda growing up together. I went into the military with his brother, Jerry Good, who was more my age. I recently found out from Tommy that Jerry ended up dying from cancer. I hated to hear that.

Bill, Jim and Rick

When Tommy visited my restaurant a few years back, he said, "You were one of the main ones that I felt I was competing against." And I said, "Tommy, you were also stiff competition." Even though we were competitors, we were also friends. He's actually 81 now, two years older than me.

The Bopsies?

We sang once at the club Gay Haven. Club Gay Haven was pretty fancy and big entertainment. It was a real honor to play there.

This was no big deal to anybody but us because nobody knew who we were. Sort of the invisible band. We got the gig because when they had off time they'd put in local groups, teen groups. They'd have teen dances, and they'd have more than one.

The 'reassembled' Tabs

That's what some of the signs are on my wall in the restaurant – they contain a list of singers who were coming, and some of the acts that were coming. However, we followed Bobby Darin. He'd just been playing there. That was a hoot.

It was during that era when we started wearing matching outfits. Everyone was doing it. Matching outfits were the big thing back then – The Temptations, The Platters, all the big-name groups wore matching outfits. We got into the matching outfits as people started booking us and we were making more money.

Madcap IV

Other than when I was singing with Jack Rainwater and the Peppermints in the beginning, when I was underage, it was always my band – always me, Rick Gambino. I know that sounds egotistical. But it was always my vision of what we would do.

When I had the band, Rick Gambino and The Other Four, I didn't want that name. The guys in the band wanted that name. I felt a little uncomfortable about that, like they were insignificant. I didn't think it was a good name, but my ego let it happen. And they didn't mind at all.

We were very popular, and we did showcases. What are showcases, you ask? Simple. We would take popular groups: The Four Lads, The Beatles, any of the groups that were popular back then, and we'd dress like them, rehearse and do their songs.

It was very popular, and we were well received. And it was a lot of fun.

Rick Gambino and the Other Four

But back to the bands.

Like most groups, I suspect, we bandmates had differences. It's human nature. Part of that was egos, part was the business itself. We decided we needed to be the best there was, even though we were considered one of the top local bands in the city of Detroit.

We were so determined to be the best (this was cruel, wasn't even my idea but I went along with it), we'd sit in chairs in a row and we'd put one of the members of the band in a chair with his back to us. We would tell him what he needed to do to get better, what he might be doing wrong that we needed to correct.

Rick Gambino
and the "Other 4"

Whoever was in the "hot seat" couldn't say anything, they couldn't defend themselves, nothing.

I remember thinking it was a little crazy. I don't remember them saying anything bad about me, except about me being a little late sometimes. The band was very complimentary and helped me be better – the more so because they were good musicians.

On the whole, I think it somehow helped the group.

Jimmy, our drummer (who was an excellent drummer), changed his last name. His real name was Jimmy Campbell and he changed it to Jimmy Lawrence. Why would you change from Campbell to Lawrence? They're both common, boring names. He would take a break and sit down in the crowd with a drum pad between his knees, talking to customers, and he'd be practicing paradiddles with his drumsticks. He was kind of like a fanatic about drumming.

I heard later that he ended up committing suicide, maybe six or seven years later.

After I pretty much left the band, they stayed intact. They didn't have a strong lead vocalist, but they did shows like they did when I was with them.

Rick Gambino
And the Other Four

The one guy in the band who was the guitar player wasn't a great guitar soloist, but he was real good at hearing the parts on songs to get us to vocally follow it. That became my job with my next group after I left them.

I became good at it, too, because it was pretty much common sense. You could pick the vocal parts from the chords in the song. It moves with the chords.

Madcap IV

I remember my bandmate who played the Cordovox (which sounded like a B3 organ). He said, "Man, we should have done everything we could to keep you in the band." I don't think they could have, because I told them I was leaving and I had plans to do something else.

God bless you guys—I loved you.

More Bands

This other group I wanted to put together was an established trio, but they were doing folk songs, like Kingston Trio stuff. "Hang Down Your Head, Tom Dooley," that kind of stuff. So, we got into more musicals and more showcases and popular stuff, like "You're Just Too Good to be True."

The 'reassembled' Tabs

We all got along real good; I can't even say that I had any favorites within any band. But we all had fun together; I don't think there was ever any animosity with the members.

I played in a number of groups. The different names included:

- *Rick Gambino and the Other Four*
- *Rick Gambino and the Reasons*
- *The United Sounds*
- *Madcap IV*

That last group I got in, the Madcap IV, we did a lot of comedy. When you get with a group that you really like and have fun with, it's easy to goof around ... play off of each other.

Money

I was the one who handled the money for the bands. The club owners usually handed it to me. I remember playing at the Village Lounge, which was one of my favorite places to play because the bar bellied out and there was a stage right behind the bar, up high – just a real good show atmosphere.

The owner was George Moran. I loved that guy. He's the guy I used to go up to and say something nice and he would repay it with an expletive.

Rick Gambino

Once, when my son Brett was with me, we went to his place. Brett went up to George and said something like, "George, man, thank you for everything," and George replied, "F... you." Brett brings that story up all the time.

I'd go up to collect the money for the band at the Village, and the band always had tabs. George would say, "This is Denny's bill," and I'd deduct his tab and figure what he got. I'd do that for Denny and then Chuck and the rest of them.

But then I'd go to pay my tab, which was as big as theirs if not bigger. George would give me my pay and I'd say, "George, where's my tab?" And he'd say, "Forget about it," or "F... you."

George always wanted me

The Vocals & Comedy of
The M A D C A P IV

to do an Italian medley for him and his girlfriend. I liked her. She was very nice. There were two things they always asked me to do for sure; one was the Italian medley and I did it in Italian.

There were parts of it, because I took it off a Jerry Vale album, in English, but most of it was in Italian and I just memorized it when I listened to the record.

The only other song I remember that she requested was "As Long as He Needs Me." If a male was singing, it was called "As Long as *She* Needs Me."

Another Story

One time we were performing at the Pink Panther club. Afterward, we went to the Rooster Tail to see Rich Little perform. Dominic (a local "connected" guy) and his entourage came in for dinner (he owned it), and he stopped by our table and said hello. He bought us all a round of drinks and some food. I felt like a big shot. When I went to thank him, he simply said, "F…k you." That's how you knew he liked you, I guess.

The Village Lounge

I remember that there was a wall at the Village Lounge, just a little knee wall, separating the bar area, which would be a separation from the bar stools and the band. The other side of the wall was about four feet high. The top of it was one-by-six, flat, and there would be the seated crowd and the dance

Rick Gambino and the Other Four

119

floor over to the left of it. I had one of the first cordless mics, it was a Shure mic. It worked pretty good for being the first of its kind.

We'd do the song "Hava Nagila," the Jewish song. And I would get off the bandstand and I would go around with the cordless mic and I would jump on that rail and I would walk down that rail. I don't know why. I was usually half in the tank when I did it. And there was that opening walkway to get to that room, and I'd easily jump across it. I can't even walk up a ladder now without hanging on.

The Madcap IV

We're talking early '60s. To make fifty bucks a night was the going rate for a top band – that was fifty bucks each – and that's the least we ever made. It would get better from there. We'd go into a bar and we drew crowds. Crowds meant liquor sales and money. A lot of times Tommy Good was down the road at the Townsman Inn.

And as I mentioned, he and I were always competing.

Some of the different clubs we played included:

- 52nd Show Bar (which had a rotating stage and was my very favorite club)

- Townsman Lounge

- Jerry's Showbar

120

- Harold's Club
- Pink Panther
- Surfside Lounge

The Surfside Lounge

The Surfside Lounge was huge, with a tall stage. We played there often. The Beatles had just come on the scene, and we did a lot of showcases there, including the Beatles. I think I played the part of Paul.

Dave DeBusschere of the Detroit Pistons was there one night. He gave me and my wife tickets to one of their games. We had special seats and shared a great time.

Gordy Howe

One day, a bunch of guys from the Detroit Lions came in, and after hours invited us to the Leland Hotel to party after the game. Since they invited me, that also included the whole band. Hall of Famer Gordy Howe of the Detroit Redwings gave me an 8"x10" black and white glossy picture that said:

To Rich from Poor, signed Gordy Howe.

Lots of fun times at the Surfside Lounge.

The Bouncer

One time, as we finished playing The Townsman Lounge and the bar was closing, there was this big Polish guy drinking at the bar. The bouncer came and told him it was 2:30 am and time to leave. The fellow was being obstinate. He started to leave, got halfway to the door, stopped, turned and came back. The bouncer jumped over the bar grabbed him and started marching him out.

Now at the Suburban Lounge . . .

RICK GAMBINO
VOCAL
and
THE AXENTS
Suburban Lounge
17575 Dix, near Oakwood, Melvindale

The guy turned and started punching the bouncer in the face, and he fell down. The guy got on top of him and kept punching. The guy wouldn't stop beating him. I couldn't understand why nobody stood up and helped. I was the smallest guy in the band, but when you see a guy that you like getting beat up, you gotta go to his aid.

So, I ran up to this big Polish fellow, and started kicking him

featuring
TOP ENTERTAINMENT
ALL YEAR LONG!

★ Dancing
Monday through Saturday
★ Twist, Limbo and
BOSSA NOVA
Every Wednesday night
Saturday nights are
★ Show Night
featuring
BILL BODIN
and the Cordiols
Plus Downriver's Newest
Recording Star,
RICK GAMBINO

COMING ATTRACTIONS!
● MARCH 23
for 2 Big Weeks
The Fabulous
FINBY FIVE
● APRIL 16
4-Week Engagement
THE HEADLINERS

Coming soon . . . DELICIOUS VENISON STEW BANQUET . . .
Everyone invited. Watch for announcement date.

Suburban Lounge
17575 Dix, near Oakwood, Melvindale

with all my might. After several kicks, he was so startled that he finally stood up. I started wildly punching him until he backed up and was out the door, and then I stopped and slammed the door shut, locking the deadbolt. I really don't know what came over me, other than what I said originally. I was helping someone I liked.

The startled looks of my bandmates at what they had just seen surprised me.

I said, "Somebody needed to help."

Nobody said a thing, but I can tell you this: I was a momentary hero, especially to the bouncer. I also suspect the band felt guilty by their response.

The Sandbox Lounge

The Sanbox Lounge was a local club in Detroit that we played. We gave a last call at 2 am and everyone had to be out by 2:30. We would usually sit around after playing and unwind with the staff and waitresses. One night, there was this guy who simply would not leave. He was harassing the servers and scaring them. A mean drunk.

I had also had a few drinks myself.

I got up in his face and told him something to the effect to get the hell out of there now or he would be sorry. Not that I could have whipped him, but I learned alcohol can make you feel tougher than you really are.

He finally ended up walking out, but not before saying "I'm gonna get a gun, hunt you down and blow your brains out."

Entertainer of the week from the Detroit News

RICK GAMBINO - This talented entertainer at the 52nd SHOW BAR, is only 25 years old. He is 5'8" tall has blue eyes and dark brown hair. His hobbies are golf and music. His favorite is the ballad, and his idol is Tony Bennett. His singing group has been together for 3 years. His favorite songs are "Shadow of your smile", "Girl Talk" and "Best Is Yet To Come". He was born in Michigan, and graduated Highland Park High School. If you enjoy very good music, played by a very talented group, don't miss Rick Gambino and the Other Four, Now playing for you at the 52nd SHOW BAR. . . .

I immediately went and got a gun permit. But back then, they told me I could only carry it in the trunk of my car, and it had to be unloaded. I thought, *If someone is gonna kill me, am I gonna say something like ... Can you hold on a minute while I get my gun out of the trunk?*

I ended up not getting a gun, figuring it wouldn't do any good unless I had a carry permit, which was almost impossible to get back then.

The guy never came back. I wonder if he even remembered saying it in the first place.

Back to the Sandbox Lounge.

This was one of the first places I played when I organized the Madcap IV. We did comedy and some show stuff. We were

Madcap IV in skit

a good vocal band, especially in harmonies. This allowed us to do a lot of show music, like "West Side Story," "Sound of Music," musicals like that. We were also able to do modern music like Mamas and Papas tunes, Four Seasons, groups like that. Tommy, my bass player, did the Frankie Valli falsetto parts of the harmony.

I was not considered a musician in those days, since I was the front man for the group. However, I did play saxophone, keyboard, guitar, and in one instance, when my six-foot-eight drummer came out front to sing the Jolly Green Giant (by the way, his height kept him out of the military), I would go back and play drums.

What I *was* proud of, however, was my ability to arrange the vocal parts for the rest of the group. I could hear what they needed to do, and was able to show it to them by singing the part.

A Temporary Storm Brewing?

While we were living at my mom's, Gari became pregnant with my second son. But problems had started to surface between us. In fact, I was contemplating divorce. It was not anything in particular, just that we fought all the time. However, by the time Brett was born, and I went to the hospital to see him, we decided to stay together.

We moved out of my mom's to Wyandotte, Michigan, and rented a house from a woman named Canigliaro. We found out her husband was part of a crime family ... or so we were told.

Incidentally, during this time, color TV was just coming out, and we watched our first show in color: *Bonanza*.

Great Telephone Service

After Brett was born, we moved to Detroit and bought a three-story house in a not-too-good section. Funny enough, it had a swimming pool in the back. All the houses butted up about two to three feet of each other, and one day I asked a contractor how they built these so close. He said from the inside out. That's how they got so close to each other. The house was on Waterman Street, just down the street from Southwestern High School.

We had a tenant on the third floor. A not-too-attractive woman. One day, she called the telephone company, and a van pulled up in front of the house. It had "Bell Telephone" painted on the side. The man went upstairs and took a long time to fix the phone. A little later, another telephone van pulled up and that man went inside, too. This went on every day for a week. It looked like a parking lot for AT&T.

Finally, Gari had had enough of that, and she got into a big argument with the tenant, who was much bigger than Gari. But when an Irish woman gets mad, you need to stay out of her way. Gari was only 115 pounds, but she would take on anybody with no fear. I had to break up the argument. I found out later the woman was paying off her bills with AT&T in the prone position.

As I mentioned, we had a swimming pool. One day, my son Rich was playing around the pool and fell in. I saw what happened and reached down and pulled him out. He coughed and sputtered, but seemed okay. I was glad as heck I was there, because he almost drowned.

Great Postal Service, Too

Gari took a job in the post office during this time and she either walked or took a bus to her job, which put her through a pretty bad part of town. I was constantly worried about her, but she never ran into any trouble, thank goodness. As I look back, I cannot believe I let her walk that short distance late at night.

Our next home was in Allen Park, which is in a much nicer area. And Adam was born there.

All during this time, I was supporting the family by playing with my various groups in the evenings and being home most of the day with Gari and the kids.

I remember when one of my sons did something wrong, many times I would have to stand them in a line until the one who committed the crime would confess. If it were today, I probably would have been charged with child abuse. I always knew where the paddle or the belt was. One time, I think Brett admitted doing something wrong when he actually didn't do it. I think he was just tired of standing at attention in a line and didn't want to snitch out the real culprit.

Our house in Allen Park had two stories. Once, when Brett was five or six years old and was walking down the stairs, he looked at us and volunteered:

"I don't have any candy in my pocket."

Turned out he did. Candy was off limits to the kids unless we gave it to them. He is much smarter than that today.

I was happy when able to spend time with my sons and played with them often. And, although my sons and I had some fun times together, looking back I wish I would have spent even more time with them.

The Vegas Deal

By 1968, I had a family of three sons – Rich, Adam and Brett. Also, in 1968 a booking agent offered the Madcap IV a gig in Las Vegas. It was pretty good money and only one downside – we would have to travel 2000 miles to get there.

We weren't a nationally known headline band – in fact, we were sort of a big fish in a small pond in Detroit. But Vegas was a lot bigger pond. They wanted us to open up for various famous headline acts that played in Vegas. This would mean uprooting my family and traveling to the state of Nevada. I discussed it with Gari, and she reluctantly said okay.

I pictured what it might be like there, and I could envision a really happy life, even if challenging. But deep inside me, something was stirring. There was something more – a voice told me there was a better option.

I sat down and listened to it.

127

Embers with Trophy

Rick and
the Other
Four

Rick and
the Other
Four

52nd SHOW BAR

Rick Gambino and the Other Four offer a musical range from blues to bop, now at the 52nd Show Bar.

Gambino band coming to Bump Shop

Rick Gambino and his son, Brett.

A unique sound will be back in town next week when musician Rick Gambino brings his band to the Bump Shop, 1695 Fort St., Lincoln Park.

Owners of the newly renovated lounge, George Moran and Johnny Kaye, say they consider it a "real coup" to have obtained Rick Gambino and Company to entertain customers Tuesdays through Saturdays, beginning at 9 p.m. Nov. 9.

"Once you hear this group, you'll know why we're so glad to have them here," said Moran — and he should know.

BACK IN THE mid to late '60s, Moran was owner of the Village Lounge Show Bar in Allen Park, where Gambino played with his group. The Showcasemen, one of the most popular groups then in the Detroit Metropolitan area. They also appeared at the Suburban Lounge, the Club Gay Haven, Thunderbowl, Surf Side Six, Geno's and the Rooster tail.

Gambino later left the group and turned his musical talents to gospel music, recording two albums. In spite of his successful career as a

vocalist, pianist and saxophonist, Gambino decided to branch out into a new area — the restaurant business.

THE LINCOLN PARK man moved to Fairhope, Ala. a resort town on the Gulf of Mexico, where he opened Gambino's, a restaurant serving Italian and American food. He later established a supper club called Rick's, which he not only owned and operated, but performed in as well.

After a fire destroyed the club recently, Gambino decided not to rebuild and put together a

new group, "Rick Gambino and Company," consisting of himself, his son Brett, on guitar and Pete Carnley, who doubles as a vocalist and bassist.

WHILE TAKING a short vacation this summer to visit his family in Lincoln Park, Gambino called on his old "boss," George Moran, at the Bump Shop.

Gambino got on stage and sang with the band that was currently playing, and was offered a job on the spot.

"He's good," said Moran of Gambino

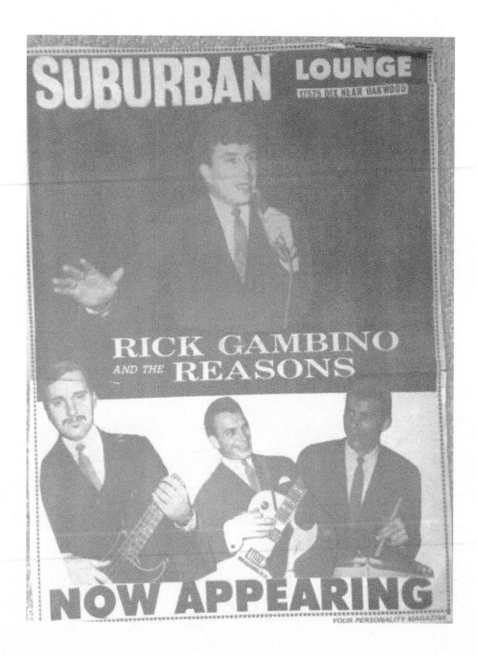

The Madcap IV

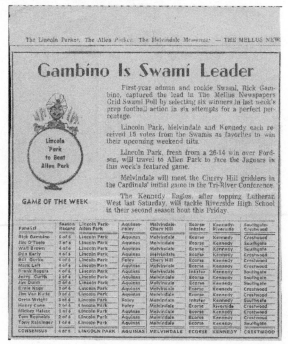

The Lincoln Parker, The Allen Parker, The Melvindale Messenger — THE MELLUS NEWS

Gambino Is Swami Leader

First-year adman and rookie Swami, Rick Gambino, captured the lead in The Mellus Newspapers Grid Swami Poll by selecting six winners in last week's prep football action in six attempts for a perfect percentage.

Lincoln Park, Melvindale and Kennedy each received 15 votes from the Swamis as favorites to win their upcoming weekend tilts.

Lincoln Park, fresh from a 26-14 win over Fordson, will travel to Allen Park to face the Jaguars in this week's featured game.

Melvindale will meet the Cherry Hill gridders in the Cardinals' initial game in the Tri-River Conference.

The Kennedy Eagles, after topping Lutheran West last Saturday, will tackle Riverside High School in their second season bout this Friday.

GAME OF THE WEEK

Panelist	Season Record	Lincoln Park-Allen Park	Aquinas-Foley	Melvindale-Chery Hill	Ecorse-Inkster	Kennedy-Riverside	Southgate-Crestwood
Rick Gambino	6 of 6	Lincoln Park	Aquinas	Melvindale	Ecorse	Kennedy	Crestwood
Jim O'Toole	5 of 6	Lincoln Park	Aquinas	Melvindale	Ecorse	Kennedy	Southgate
Walt Brown	4 of 6	Lincoln Park	Aquinas	Melvindale	Ecorse	Kennedy	Southgate
Don Early	4 of 6	Lincoln Park	Aquinas	Melvindale	Ecorse	Kennedy	Crestwood
Bill Gorke	4 of 6	Lincoln Park	Foley	Chery Hill	Ecorse	Kennedy	Crestwood
Mark Left	4 of 6	Lincoln Park	Aquinas	Melvindale	Ecorse	Kennedy	Crestwood
Jerry Curtis	3 of 6	Lincoln Park	Aquinas	Melvindale	Ecorse	Kennedy	Southgate
Frank Rogers	4 of 6	Lincoln Park	Aquinas	Melvindale	Inkster	Kennedy	Southgate
Jim Dunn	2 of 6	Lincoln Park	Aquinas	Melvindale	Ecorse	Kennedy	Southgate
Ernie Nagy	3 of 6	Lincoln Park	Aquinas	Melvindale	Ecorse	Kennedy	Crestwood
Jim Van Hurle	3 of 6	Lincoln Park	Aquinas	Melvindale	Ecorse	Kennedy	Crestwood
Orrin Wright	3 of 6	Lincoln Park	Foley	Melvindale	Inkster	Kennedy	Southgate
Henry Cone	3 of 6	Lincoln Park	Foley	Melvindale	Ecorse	Riverside	Crestwood
Mickey Halasz	2 of 6	Lincoln Park	Aquinas	Melvindale	Ecorse	Kennedy	Crestwood
Tom Reynolds	2 of 6	Lincoln Park	Aquinas	Melvindale	Ecorse	Kennedy	Crestwood
Tony Reininger	1 of 6	Lincoln Park	Aquinas	Melvindale	Ecorse	Kennedy	Southgate
CONSENSUS	4 of 6	**LINCOLN PARK**	**AQUINAS**	**MELVINDALE**	**ECORSE**	**KENNEDY**	**CRESTWOOD**

Vocals & Comedy of

THE MADCAP IV

Rick Gambino, Mgr.   Phone 388-3091

Madcap IV

Mom, Rick, cousin
Joe and his wife

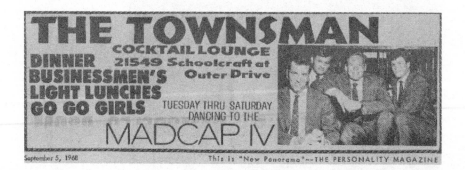

Jazz group I sang in

I did domestic things too – like cut the grass

And pose for pictures

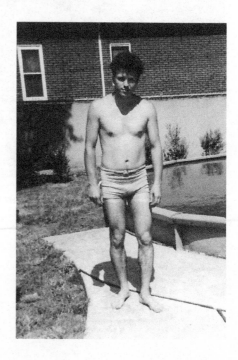

TEEN DREAM TIME *Volume 3*

32 TEEN, POP & GIRL GROUP RARITIES 1959- 1964

1. **BOBBY PEDRICK - Two Ton Tessie**
   Duel 516 (1962) (Gene Pitney- Aaron Schroeder)
2. **BETTY JAYNE - Time Will Tell**
   Mona Lee 139 (1961) (Mike Rodgers)
3. **WALLIE HAWKINS - Don't Believe Them**
   Joy 253 (1961) (Brandon- Simmons)
4. **JAN ARLEN - Certainly Love**
   Brunswick 55210 (1961) (Sid Wyche)
5. **FRANKIE CALEN - Here's Where Make Believe Ends**
   Epic 9628 (1963) (B. Raleigh- A. Wayne)
6. **RICK GAMBINO - Oh - Oh**
   Sutter 1010 (1961) (R. Gambino)
7. **PATTI BROOK - Heaven Is Being With You**
   Pye 7N.15378 (1961) (King- Goffin- Weil)
8. **LUCIEN FARRAR - Yea, Yea, Hmm, Hmm**
   Roulette 4331 (1961) (Lucien Farrar)
9. **KENNY RANKIN - Cindy Loo (My Cinderella)**
   Decca 30852 (1959) (Norman Sachs- Fred Anisfield)
10. **GEORGIANNA - I've Never, Never, Never**
    Alcor 017 -(1963) (J. Zackeary- R. Stevens)
11. **GEORGE J CAMARINOS III - Treachery**
    Buzz 109 (1960) (George J Camarinos)
12. **GRADY CHAPMAN - This, That 'n The Other**
    Mercury 71771 (1961) (Edwin Johnson- Alvin Johnson)
13. **DEBBIE REYNOLDS - Are You For Real**
    Dot 16225 (1961) (Vaughn)
14. **DANNY COUGHLAN - Oh, Such A Shame**
    Capitol 72112 (Canada) (1963) (Danny Coughlan)
15. **MOREY CARR - Meet Me Where We Used To Meet**
    Roulette 4454 (1962) (Powers- Wayne- Jordan)
16. **DIANA DARRIN - Little Gun, Little Me**
    Virgo 1005 (1961) (Sedecca- Wagner)

17. **BOBBY PEDRICK - School Crush**
    Shell 722 (1960) (H. Tobias- B. Pedrick)
18. **SANDRA THOMPSON - (My Baby Don't Love Me) No More**
    Okeh 7138 (1960) (J. DeJohn- D. DeJohn- L. DeJohn)
19. **DICK CARUSO - My One And Only Prayer**
    MGM 13052 (1961) (Greenfield- Sedaka)
20. **DOBIE GRAY - Kissin' Doll**
    Stripe 832 (1961) (Johnny Cole)
21. **JENNIE LEE LAMBERT - Hey, Mister Scientist!**
    Musicor 1010 (1961) (J. L. Lambert- R. Adams- M. Gentile)
22. **KIP PHILLIPS - Thirty- Two Girls And A Boy**
    7 Arts 716 (1961) (M. Mandel- N. Sachs)
23. **ABBY ANDERSON - (We Were) Sittin' In The Balcony**
    Knight 1047 (1964) (Lewis Lindsey)
24. **FRANKIE ANTHONY - Little Girls Have Big Ears**
    DRA 329 (1962) (H. Winn- J. Hooven)
25. **SANDY & THE SOPHOMORES - Walk Away Girl**
    Columbia 43089 (1964) (R. S. Riley)
26. **GARY LANE - How Wrong Can You Be**
    Fontana 338 (1961) (Roy Lister- Jerry Dane)
27. **ANN- MARIE - Davey**
    ABC Paramount 10418 (1963) (T. Wynn- D. Jordan)
28. **BENNY ATKINS - Campus Cutie**
    Mercury 71765 (1961) (Winfield Scott)
29. **SIMONE JACKSON - I Told You So**
    American Music Makers 002 (1963) (Collier- Denton)
30. **STANLEY LIVINGSTON - Hairspray**
    Marilyn 03 (1961) (R. Plaisted- R. Page)
31. **CLAIRETTE - Roller Coaster Romeo**
    Encore 1210 (1962) (L. Ritz- C. Randall)
32. **DENNY REED - Faithful To The End**
    Dot 16400 (1962) (C. Conway- N. Conway)

A RRR PRODUCTION 2009- These Recordings have been remastered from original vinyl sources to maintain a Dynamic Oldies Sound.

AAD   LIMITED EDITION

Back of Dream Time CD – Number 6

Never Give Up

Part Four

The Christian Years

Christian Group

The Christian Influence

Throughout my life, I have always believed in God – more often at times, less often when I was living in the material world. That was one of the times I really thought about it. What did I want to do with my life? How did I want to live it? I was always wondering what it would be like to completely surrender everything and seriously commit to a total Christian life.

The Vegas experience would surely move my career ahead. There was no telling how far we could go out there. But at what cost to me and especially to my family?

After thinking about it, I just didn't think it would have been the right thing to do, bringing my sons up in that environment. Then a feeling started to enter me. I didn't know what it was, but I imagined it to be God talking to me. I started tingling, excited. I got up and went out to my car and started driving.

The feeling became more pronounced. By giving myself to God, I started to feel invincible, as if I could do anything and it wouldn't matter. I imagine this is what my grandfather felt when Cosmo approached him in Ecorse all those years ago.

I decided that the risks were too great to go to Las Vegas. It would be totally against my Christian values and a terrible environment for my family. I shared this with my bandmates. They were extremely disappointed and asked me why. I told them the truth. I had rediscovered God and did not want to raise my family in an environment that was not consistent with Christian values. I told them they could go on without me, but they decided to disband and all went off in different directions.

I think Gari was happy with the decision, and then I had a dilemma: How could I earn a living without being in nightclubs and the righteous temptations that followed that life? I wanted to keep myself out of temptation, and after all, the church parishioners would not understand my playing in places like that.

I wanted to go all in – like I did everything I attempted in my life until then – and experience my Christian faith, and not put myself in that position.

As I look back and realize how supportive Gari was, no matter how crazy some of my ideas and venues were, I feel I always took it for granted. She was a truly remarkable lady. I would always seem to get the accolades, but the truth was she was my support system in whatever I did.

Just like me, she wasn't perfect; she could jump a person and use her high-volume voice in a way that could make you cringe. And after all of that, she would give you the shirt off her back, even if she loved that shirt.

I was blessed. She was the perfect complement to me, especially in my new commitment to Christianity.

A New Gig

After looking at various ads for jobs, I settled on a local newspaper called *The Mellus* that needed someone to sell ads. I'd never sold anything before (although selling the various bands I started to the public was a full-time job and I was good at that), but I thought I could make a go of it.

I was hired and started making sales calls. Very quickly, I caught on and was making more than enough money to keep the family going. I enjoyed it and I was home most nights to be with the kids and Gari.

More importantly, I had finally found peace within myself. An inner knowing that I was connected to God and He would look after me and my family. In a word, I was happy.

My job at the newspaper

During this period, another aspect of Christianity showed itself. When growing up I had witnessed, in a Pentecostal Church, people who spoke in tongues. I felt like maybe that would bring me closer to God. I wanted everything available in the Christian life.

I was determined not to manufacture the speaking of tongues. If I didn't receive that gift, so be it. Sometime later, after months of praying, I was in church at the altar and, wow, it came over me. It wasn't even close to what I heard other fellow Christians say. I felt renewed.

I could be driving along, and if I allowed it to happen, it happened. It was like giving everything up.

I still sometimes question the validity of what I experienced. They say that's the devil trying to tell me that. But if it wasn't real, then I have no idea what it was.

Did I miss the band? Absolutely. I loved singing. But the places I was singing were the problem. So, I sacrificed the potential career for a time. Being out of the limelight was very satisfying.

Rick with Sales staff

A few years later, the newspaper I worked for was bought out by Panax Corp., which was based in Lansing, Michigan.

I had an idea.

I called the company and asked to speak with Jack G., the President. I told him I was in sales at the paper, but that I thought I was ready to move up to manager of sales. He invited me to meet with him. I drove almost five hours there, and after a lengthy interview, he agreed to hire me as a sales manager. The job included a company car (a Buick LeSabre) and a big raise.

Praise the Lord!

Incidentally, I made most of my sales calls on my Kawasaki motorcycle, and became known as the sales guy on the motorcycle.

ADVERTISING STAFF—Rick Gambino, David Garland and Richard Bauer.

Rick at newspaper with sales staff

An employee who worked for me approached me for some advice. He said "Rick, I just can't seem to sell up to the standards of the rest of the staff. I'm unable to get the results."

Appointments named on Record-Leader ad staff

I ended up taking the job of the guy on the left, too.

I told him he needed to make two or three times as many calls as he was making. In other words, he had to work much harder than the rest of the team in order to make his goals. He appreciated that and later did quite well. It was advice I would need to rely on most of my life as well.

With the new job, I moved to Ithaca and found a home. It was a house, barn and chicken coop on twenty acres, which was part of a larger parcel of eighty acres.

I should mention here that I had a German Shepherd at the old house, and that he was very attached to me. I found out he was locked down in the basement because he was getting too aggressive without my being there. Gari was afraid to go down and do the laundry. I traded that dog for a new one. I finally moved the family

Rick on the farm

(and my new dog, a St. Bernard) to the new home, and we settled in.

Rick, Advertising Manager; Marty, General Manager; and Dick, Editorial Manager

During this time, I found time to spend with my family, and three growing sons. I built various things, including a swing set, we played ball in the yard, and I bought them all bikes. Later, I

would coach them in basketball and other sports. I wish I had done more. I didn't have much of an example of how to be a father since my dad left the family when I was eight. He was a great man but old-school Italian.

One of the pleasant surprises while working at the newspaper was meeting Dave, who had a quartet that played in places like the American Legion, weddings and other basically non-alcoholic themed venues. I was then able to

Christian singing group

do my music on weekends and keep a harmonious family life.

I got the job because they needed a keyboard player. I could play basic chords, so I bought a Lowery organ. I had a Ford Econoline van at the time, the kind with the engine between the seats. I would set the organ behind the seats and drive it around (it was a full-size organ, with pedals).

Eventually, they discovered that I could sing, and we added that element to the band.

Spanish American Christian Crusades

We were going to church and participating in various church activities in our new community. The sister of one of my bandmates was married to a guy in another Christian band called the Spanish American Christian Crusades. I found there was an opening for a keyboard player in this band and asked if I could join. They agreed. It's not like I was a great piano player, but I could pound out a number of chords and make up the rest as we went along. I have a decent ear and good relative pitch, so it was easier to pick up the various chords.

During this time, I was manager of classified advertising for two small newspapers: *Mount Pleasant Times* and the *Daily Record Leader*. Eventually, I became manager in charge of all ad sales for the newspapers. A lot of responsibility. I did well at it. And, as I mentioned, I was very happy there and in my life in general.

But something was bubbling in the background. Perhaps another calling?

I was playing in Dave's quartet, and also playing in various churches with the new group. It became apparent that the Spanish American Christian Crusades was going to take all of my time if I committed to it. I had to make a decision. My heart was in the Christian music and lifestyle, so I finally decided to quit my job and go all in with my Christian music and the Spanish American Christian Crusades.

We started getting bookings at churches, which provided an income. When we traveled, the church's parishioners always put us up at one of their homes. We traveled a lot, and I took the family whenever I could. Otherwise, they stayed home at the house on the farm.

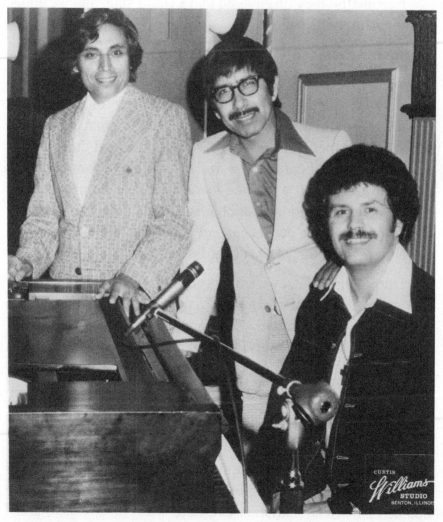

Spanish American Christian Group Luz Gonzales, Simon Avila and Rick

Travelin' Van

A church where we went to play asked what our plans were. We told them we were hoping to spread our particular form of gospel far and wide, but transportation was a problem. All the members pitched in money and they bought us a brand-new van. It was super.

EL NORTE

Later, the band asked if I would take a job on my own and go to Monterrey, Mexico. We ended up using the van. I packed the whole family in it, and we drove all the way down there. It was close living, all of us living and sleeping in one van. After a couple of weeks, we headed back home to Michigan, and I think the whole family was glad to be back.

Cruise Ship

A large church wanted to take a cruise to the Bahamas and needed a religious music group to go along. I was able to bring the family on this adventure. It was a great trip. The family really enjoyed it. However, one incident stands out.

As Gari and I were returning from a shore excursion on the bus, an older couple exited a little in front of us. The bus had parked very close to the edge of the pier, and as the woman got out, she somehow tripped and went over the side. The husband looked over at her, turned, and started screaming for help, running after us as we were walking away. He was shouting that his wife had fallen into the water.

I ran up to the dock and looked over. She was down maybe twenty-five feet and looked like she was struggling to stay afloat. She managed to stay above water and still hold on to her purse strap. Although not the best of swimmers, I felt compelled to jump in after her as I saw no other help. I quickly pulled off my shoes and was getting ready to jump in. Gari was yelling at me not to do it, and to tell the truth, I was not happy about jumping down there. Fortunately, there were two Jamaican kids who saw it all and one of them jumped in and pulled her to safety.

I'm not sure what I was thinking, but I am glad they helped before I jumped in.

The Album

Another congregation that we played for decided that we were good enough to make an album, and that by offering the record for sale at the various church concerts, we could make more money and help spread the gospel. So, they paid for Simon and me to each make our own album. They paid for the whole works: studio time, musicians, cover artwork and pressings.

We went to Queen City Records in Cincinnati to do the recording. Across the bridge in Covington, Kentucky, was a small hotel, and we decided to stay there

Rick recording album
Queen City Records
Cincinnati, Ohio

for the night before recording the next morning. I was keyed up, excited and nervous.

150

Unfortunately, the room next door had a wedding reception and the whole group was out on the patio whooping it up. It was all I could do not to break my commitment to Christianity and bring up some verbiage I

Rick's Album

had not used in a long time. We asked the hotel to move us to a different location, but all the rooms were filled. So, I laid on my bed, seething, and stared at the ceiling all night.

When I arrived at the studio the next morning, I had not slept for one minute the previous twenty-four hours. I recorded the album anyway. I was not a coffee drinker, but that day I drank many cups of the caffeinated ooze to try and keep awake.

Honestly, the lack of sleep compromised my performance on the album. I was pushing too hard and felt like I didn't sing my best. The musicians came in and laid the tracks down, and I came in after them and sang. I recorded Frank Sinatra's "My Way", only changing the words to "God's Way", and I wrote a complete song.

Simon did very well on his album, and he sounded great. The good news of it all was we had albums to sell at our church gigs and that improved our income even more.

Even though I feel because of the lack of sleep I didn't come close to what I felt was my best effort, I have loaded the album on my website, and you can listen to it for free there.

Sleepwalking

Once, when we played at a church, I was staying upstairs in a parishioner's older home. I should mention that I never sleepwalk and generally am a pretty sound sleeper.

I had a terrible dream in which I felt the house falling fast like in a huge landslide, and felt I had to get out. I ran to the window, stepped out onto a roof overhang and walked the eight feet or so to the edge. Looking down, I could see what I thought were pillars of some sort. I didn't want to jump and land on them, so I walked back.

While climbing through the window, I suddenly woke up and found myself halfway through it. Sleepwalking. It was not a dream. I was actually outside, and I did go to the edge and look down. It frightened me. I went back to bed.

Next morning, I went outside to see what the pillars were that I had seen the night before while sleepwalking. Turns out they were tall skinny shrubs and bushes. I shudder to think what would have happened had I actually jumped.

Nothing like that has ever happened again.

Saved by the Vitamin Bottles

At another church gig, I was put up in a home on the second floor. But the stairs to my room also went into the host couple's bedroom, right next to their bed. I must have drunk too much iced tea, because in the middle of the night I had to go to the bathroom, and it was down the stairs, right next to their bed, and right through their bedroom. I didn't want to wake them up.

Then I had an idea. I emptied a number of my vitamin bottles, shook out the pills and … uh … filled them up. It was enough to allow me to wait for morning to go to the bathroom.

I am pretty sure I did not reuse those bottles.

Left Behind

Simon and I were returning from a gig we performed in the South, and we were using a self-contained camper, the kind that had the bed over the driver's cab. I was sleeping in the bed when, halfway through Tennessee, Simon stopped to gas up the motorhome. I got out and went to the bathroom, telling Simon I would drive the last half of the journey.

When I returned from the restroom, the gas was in the car and I thought Simon was in the loft bed, sleeping above me. I started the van and took off.

After a number of hours, I thought it strange Simon wouldn't have said anything, so I called out his name. No answer. I stopped the motorhome and looked above, only to find an empty bed. No Simon. Then it hit me. I must have left him behind at the gas station. I knew if I drove back, he would be gone, and I wasn't even sure I could remember where I had left him. So, I continued on to Michigan (this was way before cell phones).

I found out later he took a flight home. I felt pretty bad about it, but it worked out okay in the end. Once back together, we all had a great laugh about it.

The Dinner Napkin

I was at an event put on by the Christian churches and there were hundreds of people in attendance. We had a lovely dinner, and then the ceremonies began. Partway through, they called me up to speak, and I got up from the table and walked to the front of the auditorium.

Gari kept yelling at me. *What? I thought.* I turned and she pointed to my belt. I looked down and there was the dinner napkin, hanging down to my knees. I quickly pulled it away, somewhat too late since I had already walked past several rows of people, and made my way to the front, to the delight and laughter of the audience.

Did that Really Happen?

Once, I came home from lunch as I normally did, and went out to the barn where my 200-pound dog Alfie was chained. He wasn't a mean dog, just somewhat hard to control. I would lie down and would beat my chest, a sign for him to stand over me, and then I'd pet him rigorously.

Alfie is the culprit

Suddenly, I felt water in my mouth. I looked up to see if it was rain, but there was not a cloud in the sky. Then I looked down and there was water dripping from his God-given relief valve. A very unusual lunch, to say the least.

154

Darn dog. Maybe I needed my old German Shepherd back. And by the way, if anyone is curious, I can testify firsthand that dog pee has no taste.

The Mysterious Animal in the Tree

One of the learning experiences for us was getting used to being in the country – after all, we were city folks from Detroit. One night, while we were in bed, we heard what sounded like a small animal in the front of the house. It kept me awake for hours.

Furious, I got up and grabbed my brother's three-gauge shotgun which I had gotten after he died, went out the front door in my undies and listened. It seemed like it was coming from a large tree. But it was dark, so I couldn't see anything. I aimed where I thought the sound came from and fired. Dead silence. Yes, I thought. Got it.

Kids in Michigan

I turned to go back in the door, and it started again. I raised the gun and fired again. The sound stopped. Maybe I winged it last time. Now it must be dead. After a few moments it started again. I gave up, went in the house and told Gari it, whatever it was, had won. I was also running out of ammo.

We found out later it was a katydid.

A long-horned grasshopper.

Not sure why I have included this story, but I promised myself I would include everything significant in my life, including the good, the bad, and sometimes the … stupid.

The Wrestling Bear?

Up in Michigan, there was a fair with all kinds of events including log rolling. The part of it that is involved in this story is the bear wrestling. They had this bear you could put your name in and wrestle him. My wife's brother tried to wrestle the bear and got thrown across the yard. The next guy was a lumber jack type of guy, maybe three hundred pounds of fat and muscle, and he was thrown across the yard right away.

Then it was my turn. I went in, standing up, and made contact. He would try and move me down, but I wouldn't go down. The last time I went at him, I broke away and came back at him, he reached down and grabbed my ankle and tripped me to the ground. I lost.

But I outlasted the others.

I have a film of it that I am posting to the website you can see.

Rat in the Farmhouse

We were in bed getting ready to go to sleep. Then we noticed a huge rat about the size of a squirrel run across the floor and scurry behind the dresser. I was within arm's reach of the closet and grabbed the pellet gun. I told Gari if she got up and pulled the dresser out, I could get a shot at the rat. It took me a

Rick with friends Joel and Larry
Catching brown trout

minute or two to convince her. I could tell she didn't want to do it. But she got up, grabbed the back of the dresser and the rat came flying out, big as a squirrel, to the corner of the room as I was sighting it. Suddenly, it seemed to fly almost halfway up the wall. I took a quick bead on him and pulled the trigger. One shot. Got him. Hit him square in the head.

It fell to the floor. I smiled at Gari and pretended to blow the smoke off the end of the gun, gunfighter style. I promise you. It was just a lucky shot.

Worst part was picking it up and moving it out of the house. I was always tentative about that kind of stuff.

Living in the country did have its interesting times.

The Opera Singer

Interestingly, after I was in the service, I met a guy named Rich B. who was in the army too. When he got out, we hung out together off and on and kept in touch through the years. He learned to hypnotize people while in the service. One time, he said he could teach me how to hypnotize someone, using the mother method. I was intrigued and said sure.

Rich Brisbois

He hypnotized Gari using the method. She was petite and was also easy to hypnotize. When he told her that her arm was frozen, the two of us could not move it. He then had her stiffen up and put her head and feet on the backs of chairs. You could almost sit on her. It was amazing. He tried to hypnotize me, but it did not work.

He taught me how to do it. The method I preferred was the mother method that he used, where you would touch different parts of their body, getting them to relax.

Sometime later, there was a party at my house, and an extremely shy, nice-looking woman volunteered to be hypnotized. I hypnotized her using the relaxing/touch method, told her she was a famous opera singer, and brought her out to the party where everyone was congregating. She started to sing, very operatic, and everyone started laughing. She thought she was in Carnegie Hall doing opera.

My brother and mother walked in just as she started bawling hysterically. I guess even the great opera singers would cry if their audience started laughing during a serious opera aria. I rushed up to get her out of it, but nothing I did pulled her out of the hypnotic state. I tried everything Rich had taught me.

I had to call Rich, who lived a short way away, and he rushed over and finally got her out of it. He said, "One, you're this, two, now you're coming out, and three, you're awake."

I wanted to be out of the hypnosis business after that. Too dangerous. But people loved it. I still did it a few more times at parties, with no negative incidents.

Oh No, Not Again

One last point about this – a little déjà vu, if you will. Rich invited us over to his house for a party. At the end of the night, instead of everyone driving home after too much to drink, he invited all of us to stay the night. However, he wanted me to sleep in his bed. So, I did. And then the same old thing ... creeping hands appeared. I just rolled over and I guess he took the hint.

It never came up again. But then again, I never slept over at his house again either.

Cristo Brothers

My father-in-law, Gari's Dad Jim, was a handyman/contractor who worked for a large company building churches and schools in Michigan. He was always complaining about not having his own business, and once he approached me about helping him get some jobs. I was a good salesman, so after talking with Gari I accepted. The deal was 50/50 ownership. I would sell jobs and he would build. After getting some idea of what we were to do, I went out and hit the streets. The first job I sold was a complete remodel.

When I told him about it, he said he did not have enough people to work that and the other jobs, and I found myself slinging a sledgehammer to demolish some walls. *What am I doing this for? I thought. I am going out to get the job. Maybe someone else should be tearing down the walls.*

I told Jim my feelings and continued selling jobs.

321 West Center Street
ITHACA, MICHIGAN 48847

Then he came by the house one day and said he wanted to talk with me about something that was bothering him.

"What is it?" I asked.

"Well, I am not happy with the arrangement we have, as far as the percentage of ownership is concerned."

"Really, what about that arrangement?"

"I think it should be 51% to me, and 49% to you."

That really pissed me off.

As I said, he was complaining about not having enough business, and I came on and brought him more than he could do. And now he wanted 51% of the thing?

I told him I would think about it, but I had already made up my mind. I spoke with Gari, since it was her father, and she agreed it was greedy and really not fair in the least. I got back with him and shared with him not only was I not going to agree to that deal, there was no deal. I was through being his partner. We ended up on good terms.

I hated that it happened because it was Gari's father. Sometimes you have to stand up for what you believe is right, no matter who it is.

My Father Moves

In 1971, after my dad retired from Ford after forty years, he wanted to live near Gari, me and the family, so he bought a house in St. Louis, Michigan, which was about ten minutes from us.

From the start, he didn't like it there. He wanted a garden, and the winters were horrendously cold, with snow up to your knees, he would say. Finally, he had had enough and decided to move somewhere he could have a garden

Dad and family

and no snow. He was born in Flatcreek, Alabama, so he started in the state of Alabama. His research and readings convinced him that Fairhope, Alabama, was one of the top ten retirement destinations and would be the best place to retire – it met all of his requirements.

He asked me to come down to Alabama with him, and I did. After exploring the area, he bought what used to be an inn and a nursing home. Originally, it was called the Sunset Inn. Some people in the know say Elvis stayed there before he was discovered. Could be.

I liked the area, too. It was friendly, clean and affordable.

Dad's house in Fairhope, Alabama

Interior of Dad's house

I Move

I traveled back home to Michigan and got a job at Sears selling appliances, which gave me enough money to continue my gospel singing without putting the family in financial risk. I was still deep with Christ in my life, and wanted everything to work – family and career. We also had my son Josh and another on the way.

But there were clouds on the horizon.

As I said, I liked Fairhope and knew that my dad, although happy with his choice, still missed us. However, there were problems between Gari and me, and I reasoned in the back of my mind something would soon have to give. I thought going to Alabama would be a short-term solution and give me a chance to work things out with Gari and the family. I guess I was just escaping.

My managers at Sears were very supportive and allowed me to transfer to the Sears in Mobile, Alabama, in the same department (appliances), which I hoped would be my final destination. I told Gari I was going and would send for them, and I took off alone. Surprisingly, I felt a burden lift from me. I wondered if I would send for the family, and if my marriage would survive.

I had a lot of thinking to do.

Mobile and Beyond

After arriving in Mobile, I had a lot to do. First, I had to buy a car, which I did for fifteen dollars. It was a Mercury, and a clunker, but it got me around. Then I needed a place to stay close to work. I found a room above a garage on Monterey Street in downtown Mobile.

I was working my job in appliances at Sears while looking for somewhere I could sing at night.

There was a Chinese restaurant called the Chinese Palace, and they were remodeling their bar into a nice lounge. I convinced them to hire me to sing. But … I needed a piano.

Ad from Sears in newspaper

One of the connections I'd made in the Christian group was with a piano dealer in Michigan. I introduced myself over the phone, and they remembered me. I didn't mention I was no longer in the ministries. I negotiated buying a brand-new baby grand Kawai for $2,700 and told them I needed it delivered to the Chinese Palace in Alabama. They did it, with no charge for delivery.

I started playing at the lounge and soon realized that I could eventually make enough money playing music. That meant I would not need to keep my job at Sears, so after about six months I quit and went all in with my music. I started singing in several piano bars like Papa George's, the Lighthouse and many others. I had a guy named Senne B. move the piano from bar to bar for fifty dollars.

The music in Mobile was going well, and I liked the lifestyle of a musician and being on my own. There was this place right down the street from me called Big Daddy's (not the same one in Fairhope today) and they paid me twenty-five bucks a night, which was not a lot of money but okay for the 1970s. But there were tips on top of that. Also, by that time I had moved into a rental at my dad's and had a place of my own.

I would talk to Gari and the kids often, but when the question of when I was coming home or when they were coming to join me came up, I was evasive and non-responsive.

Apparently, she and the family had had enough.

I finally got *the* call.

"Hello," I answered the phone.

"Hey, Richard, it's Gari. When are you coming home?"

"Don't know," I said. "Things are going pretty well here."

Truth was, I was not planning on going back home. Things between Gari and I were tense when I left, and I was seriously considering separating. Eventually.

"What are you saying?" she asked.

"I am not saying anything. It's just, I don't know when."

"We, we need you to come home."

I could hear frustration in her voice. I didn't blame her. She was raising the boys and I knew it was tough. Next thing I heard was a click and she hung up. The phone rang a few minutes later.

"Yeah," I answered. It was Brett.

"Hey, Dad. You mean you're not coming home?"

That did it. A chord was struck deep within me. I thought back to my dad leaving when I was eight, and then thought of my sons growing up without a dad. I couldn't live with myself. I couldn't let him or my other sons down. It was tearing at me. I made a decision on the spot.

"Brett, I'll come home soon."

At Daily Record-Leader

Gambino named ad manager

RICK GAMBINO

ALMA--Rick Gambino has been named Retail Advertising Manager of the Daily Record-Leader. The announcement was made today by Martin N. Heim, Regional Manager for Panax Corporation's Central Division, which includes Gratiot County's only daily newspaper.

Gambino, 30, has been on the staff of the Daily Record-Leader since Nov. 1970. During that time he has served as Classified Advertising Manager and display salesman. He will continue in his role as classified manager in addition to his new responsibilities.

Prior to his arrival in Alma last year, Gambino was a display advertising salesman with the Mellus Newspapers in Lincoln Park. Mellus is one of the largest and most successful weekly newspaper organizations in the country. During his sales career, Gambino was also a sales representative for the Crawford Broadcasting Company, in Detroit.

Before he decided on a sales career, Gambino was a professional entertainer. He spent nine years in show business as a band leader, agent, arranger, singer and musician. He has appeared on stage, radio and television throughout the U.S.

Regional Manager Heim had this to say about Gambino, "Rick is not new to us. He's been with Panax for the past three years and his success in advertising has been

nothing less than phenomenal. He is probably one of the finest young advertising persons that I have seen in quite some time. His selection for the total advertising responsibility here in Alma was unanimous.

"Rick's knowledge of retail sales, promotion and programming plus his lively approach will be an asset in the local retail market. Rick Gambino is a live-wire. Ask anyone who knows him!"

The new advertising manager was born in Detroit. He graduated from Lincoln Park High School and entered the Army before embarking on his career in show business. In high school he played football and bowled. For the past two seasons he has been a member of the Daily Record-Leader bowling team. In the summer he plays softball in the Gratiot County Church League. He also enjoys music, painting and singing.

Gambino and his wife purchased a farm at 345 Olson Road . . . a lifelong city dream that became reality a few months back. The young couple has three boys, ages 8, 7 and 3.

Rick Gambino was also a member of the Daily Record-Leader display staff that was recently awarded the Michigan League of Home Dailies No. 1 advertising award . . . a distinction awarded annually to only two of 22 Michigan daily newspapers. It was the second consecutive year that the Daily Record-Leader captured the coveted advertising plaque.

HOME AND FOREIGN MINISTRIES

PRAY WITHOUT
CEASING

Birthdates:
Rick—April 28
Gari—November 30
Rich—May 30
Brett—October 30
Adam—October 4
Josh—April 14
Luke—May 7

Home Address:
321 W. Center
Ithaca, Michigan
48847
Phone 517-875-3632

PRAISE THE LORD

THE GAMBINO FAMILY
Rich, Josh, Rick, Adam, Brett, Luke, Gari

166

Mom smiling

First Christian Singing group in Alma, Michigan

My sister Serena

I also tried my hand at painting

Van used for Lowry organ

Our big red barn on the farm

Never Give Up

Part Five

From Pasta Perfection to
Dreams Up in Smoke

The Gambino Family

Coming to Mobile

I flew home from Mobile to Detroit and started the process of moving. A year earlier, I had sold the farm and bought a little house in Ithica. We sold that and all the furniture, packed up everything we could into a little U-Haul trailer, and drove south to Alabama in a huge, used, four-door Oldsmobile, with $5,000 to our name.

It's a miracle we made it.

We rented an apartment on my dad's property in Fairhope and I continued playing the lounges in the area, garnering a reputation and a following. I finally ended up at Baron's Restaurant and Lounge, which was managed by John B. It was a small bar and people were filling it up every night, but across the hall the restaurant was dead every night.

That's a Pizza

Even though things were going well at the bar, I started to feel that I did not want to be playing piano like that forever. The idea of a pizza joint intrigued me. I had never been in the food business before, and had no idea what was involved, but the thought of being my own boss and taking control of my, and our family's, future, appealed to me. I scouted around and finally eyed a potential location that seemed ideal. The place was closed.

I called the owner of the Parker House Motel and Restaurant who said he had just leased it to a fellow who was going to open up … a pizza place. They say timing is everything. I put it out of my mind for the moment, and continued playing at the Baron's Lounge.

The Baron's Restaurant and Lounge was built and owned by two businessmen – one named Jack, who owned a car dealership in Daphne, and another named John, who was in the insurance business. They originally built the motel, restaurant and bar as an investment and had managers running the place. As I mentioned, I was filling up the bar every night, and they were pleased with the results. A large part of the clientele were wealthy Fairhopians who spent money and were loyal.

I had always thought the name for my pizza restaurant would be Gambino's Pizza. One day, I was driving by the pizza location I had been interested in, and it was open. I was shocked by the name the owner chose—it was so close to the name I had envisioned. He called it BamaBino's Pizza, which, as you can imagine, was pretty close sounding to Gambino's Pizza.

I went inside and introduced myself. I shared how he had beat me out, and asked how he was doing. The place looked to me like it was not doing well at all. I looked around and could understand why. He was serving food in the frozen aluminum containers they came in, not even emptying them onto a plate.

He suggested maybe I could be partners with him. I said no thanks, wished him well and walked out. I figured his business was on a death spiral, and I didn't want to become involved with that.

On another front, there was still Baron's Restaurant where I was playing in the bar. But, before I knew what was happening, John and Jack had leased it to a fellow named Fender (I liked to call him Freddie Fender), who was a cook in the armed forces before taking over the restaurant. I thought, "Damn, I missed out on this one, too."

Fender was a pretty negative guy. Every time I ran into him, he would say, "Oh, I lost $800 last night." It was constant. I didn't understand how he could stay in business and advertise to customers how much he was losing nightly. I figured he was on borrowed time and I would have to wait him out.

On a funny note (more like tragic, actually), his daughter, who was the bartender, kept the expensive liquor for the bar in the trunk of her car. She would run out to get it when someone ordered a drink. Fender was paranoid about leaving the high-dollar booze in the bar.

Very weird.

The Question

Months passed. I guess the bug of owning my own business had gotten firmly entrenched in me, and I set my sites on Baron's Lounge and Restaurant, since Fender, the guy who leased it, had defaulted and was out of the picture. It was a lot bigger than the bar, and I had no experience in the restaurant business. I had never even been inside a restaurant kitchen.

I approached John and Jack and asked them if I could lease the lounge and restaurant. They thought it over for a couple of days and said yes. It would cost me $4,000 per month to lease everything.

I then asked the one question that I think, for all intents and purposes, changed my life.

"Would you consider selling and financing the restaurant to me?"

They thought about it and said yes. They told me the price and said they would take $10,000 down and the payments would be $2,500 per month – $1,500 per month less than leasing it. Go figure. My Christian life seemed to be helping me.

I know this car dealer and insurance man were smart and intelligent people, but I still to this day don't understand the lease versus purchase price they gave me. I wasn't complaining. In fact, I was elated.

I talked it over with Gari, and she agreed it would be a good idea. But where to get the money? That's when I approached my father.

The Money

"Dad, I really don't want to be a piano player in a lounge the rest of my life."

He looked at me and nodded his head.

"I have an idea. The opportunity of a lifetime. I've got the owners to agree to sell me the restaurant."

"How does it work?"

"The price is $160,000. They've agreed to let me put $10,000 down and then make payments. Could you loan me the $10,000?"

"How do I get paid back?"

"From the profits. You'd be first in line."

He thought about it. He had a way of taking his time before answering tough questions.

"Dad. I can make this work. I know how to make it a success."

He finally said yes and gave me the money. He also helped by working in the back and taking care of the money, and he loved mopping occasionally – in part, I suspect, to make sure he did get paid back. Which he did.

He paid himself back in a very short time.

Much later, I ended up selling the restaurant and gave my dad a $30,000 bonus, in addition to paying back the original loan. I found out later he was a little disappointed in me – not for the amount of money, but because he wanted to continue being part of the restaurant. I had no idea and was totally unaware of this thought of his. I thought he was happy about how it all turned out.

The reason I did all of this was because in the back of my mind I wanted to do more. I enjoyed the venture of a new place more than operating it. I had an internal goal.

Dad and Rick

The Early Gambino Years

As the new owner of Baron's, I had to make a decision as to what it would be. On the one hand, my roots were Italian, and I wanted to make a great Italian restaurant. But we were also in Alabama, and that meant seafood. So, I made a critical decision: I would split the menu in two. Half of the items would be Italian, and half would be seafood. There were also Italian/seafood combinations.

The kitchen was huge, so I split it into two parts also. On one end, I made seafood and American dishes, and all the fish that went with it. At the other end, Italian. I needed an Italian cook, so I went to Mobile to an Italian restaurant called Caesars and met a guy who said he would come over and take over the Italian side of the cooking. Great.

He and the prep cooks were on one end.

I knew of another fellow named Herbert who worked at the Sheraton in Mobile, but he also had a little grocery store in

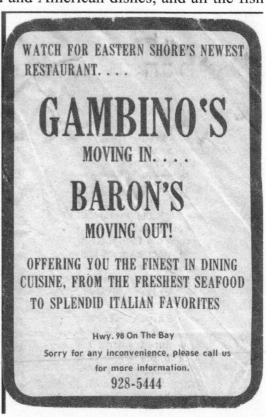

WATCH FOR EASTERN SHORE'S NEWEST RESTAURANT. . . .

GAMBINO'S

MOVING IN. . . .

BARON'S

MOVING OUT!

OFFERING YOU THE FINEST IN DINING CUISINE, FROM THE FRESHEST SEAFOOD TO SPLENDID ITALIAN FAVORITES

Hwy. 98 On The Bay
Sorry for any inconvenience, please call us
for more information.
928-5444

Fairhope. He was great with seafood, so I hired him, and he ran the seafood side of the grill. I told him I wanted a working chef.

Turned out, he sat in a chair most of the time. That was one of the first lessons I learned. No chefs. Hire only cooks.

Unfortunately, the Italian side of the grill was not working. We had problems almost from day one. The food was not up to my – or anybody's – standards. After checking a bit more, I discovered that the cook was really a dishwasher, not a cook at the restaurant I hired him from. So, I fired him.

I then had to create the menu, of course with Gari's input. With my sales and layout experience from the newspaper jobs in Michigan, I was able to slap one together. The original menu is still in the lobby of Gambino's.

Page 12-A EASTERN SHORE COURIER, Thursday, May 13, 1976

Gambino's Ready To Serve

Gambino's Restaurant is now serving hungry residents of the Eastern Shore with an Italian cuisine. Formerly Baron's Restaurant, the interior has undergone extensive remodeling and features live dinner music. Enjoying the new atmosphere are (seated) Rick and Rocco Gambino and, standing, Beulah Gambino and Jan Nobis.

We also had customer service and satisfaction problems. We were brand new. I remember many times running out into the parking lot after people who were unhappy with their meals and I would apologize about the food and ask them to give us another chance. I told them we were new, that we were going to work it out. And we started to create a small but loyal following.

I still had a major problem. I needed an Italian cook.

I took a trip to my hometown in Michigan to get a cook I had heard was good. He did not want to move to Fairhope, but he introduced me to another cook, a skinny African American, who agreed to come down and take over the Italian part. The good news was he would do things the way we wanted him to. The food improved tremendously, and people started commenting about the quality of the food. At last.

Lorenzo from Michigan

Once, we had to separate the two sides of the kitchen because the seafood side was unhappy with the Italian side. One of the guys in seafood pulled a knife on the other side. Since I had no previous experience, I wondered if this was normal. I hoped not.

Finally, the two sides and the food worked themselves out, and things were running fairly well

Gambino kitchen

Gari was doing all the bill paying, licensing and permits. We were learning the restaurant business on the fly. Our kids would come in after school and do their lessons in the office. Gari would feed them there. Not an Ozzie and Harriet lifestyle.

Early Gambino's interior

I remember more than once running checks up to the bank to cover others we had written. We always made it, but it was close.

In spite of all the trials and tribulations, I finally started to reap some benefits from the restaurant, and I was feeling pretty good about the decision to purchase it.

The Buyer

It was about a year later in 1977 or 1978, and we were doing a great business. We focused on providing value for the money, and the quality of the food. It was paying off. The customers were finally coming in and increasing every week. I was singing and playing in the bar, and everything was running smoothly.

The first time I met Grover was when someone said there was a fellow who wanted to talk with me. I said sure. We were pretty busy, and he quickly said he liked the operation, and asked if I would be interested in opening up another Gambino's.

"Why not just invest in this one?" I suggested.

"Sure," he said. "That would be fine."

I told him I would figure as honestly as I could a fair market value for the land and business, and eventually offered him thirty percent of the business in stock. He bought the stock, and I could finally relax a little, having a nest egg and the business as well.

It's Not My Job

When I played piano in the bar, I always dressed well, usually in a suit and tie. One day, a server from the kitchen came up and told me there was a problem with the dishwasher. I went into the kitchen and asked, "What's the problem?"

"The dishwasher is not putting the dishes where they belong on the shelves," I was told.

I asked the dishwasher why he didn't do that.

"It is not my job to do that."

"Well," I said, "you're right. It is not your job. You're fired. You don't have a job."

You can just imagine who ended up washing the dishes. I grabbed an apron, donned it, and started washing the dishes and putting them in the correct area after they were cleaned. From piano bar to dishwasher in five minutes.

I know for certain that night we had the best-dressed dishwasher in the area.

The Breakup

Grover ended up dating my mom, which was a little weird. He even wanted to marry her. I was against it and told him to "forget about it." We took trips together. Gari and I would often go to New Orleans with him and my mom, and generally would have a good time with him.

One time, we even went to New York to see a restaurant he liked called the Carriage Club, an upscale tablecloth place. It

was a big venue for people who wanted to be discovered, because the servers would sing, and it was the hot spot for theatre music wannabes. I enjoyed the place.

Things went along well for a while, but little things with Grover started to get my attention. Nothing overt. Mostly looks and short snappy answers which were inappropriate. One time, I was rehearsing a song with the house band in the lounge and

Grover and my Mom

he just glared at me, with daggers in his eyes. I jumped off stage, ran up to him and asked what was going on.

"You don't put that kind of music in here," he said.

That really pissed me off. This was my end of the business and I knew what I was doing.

"I'll sing whatever I want!" I shouted back.

It escalated until he started shouting in the lobby. I told him we should take it outside because customers were hearing it. We took it outside into the gravel parking lot, continuing to shout the entire time. He was bumping me with his hands, pushing me away from him. He grabbed my gold chain I had around my neck (we can all remember those days).

Something inside me snapped.

"Oh, you want to push, huh?!" I shouted.

I pushed him back hard and he fell to the ground, skinning himself up. He got back up, spied my wife Gari going to her car on the other side of the lot and ran over to her. I followed behind him. He ran up to her and started yelling, pointing his finger in her face. I could see the fear in her eyes.

Rick's first band at Gambino's
The Townsman

I caught up with him, grabbed his finger, yanked it, and he screamed. He went to Thomas Hospital to get it fixed. Maybe it was broken or sprained, I didn't care. He had crossed the line and I couldn't take it anymore.

After some thought and discussion with Gari, I subsequently asked Grover to go for a ride in the car to get some privacy. I suggested one of us had to go. The business partnership was not working. I told him I didn't have the money to buy him out, so why didn't he buy me out. He said okay.

I gave him a sweetheart deal, just to get away. I sold Gambino's lock stock and barrel. It took a few weeks to complete, and I walked away with cash in hand, knowing I was better off on my own. I felt free.

I then saw a new place that really interested me.

I envisioned a whole new concept

And a new name.

My First Venture

Flush with the money from the sale of Gambino's to Grover, I started planning my next move. I had been keeping an eye on a little place that used to be called the Supper Club and the Red Light. It was currently called the Alamo. It was a biker bar, and it was in need of everything. I went in it one time and thought if I didn't leave real soon, I would be killed. Guys with tattoos, bikers that looked like death on wheels.

But, I thought, it was a fantastic location, right on 104 with plenty of parking. I could see the potential, and given the right remodel, it could be everything I dreamed of. I tracked down the owner and bought it.

My thinking went like this.

The big rage at the time was the movie Urban Cowboy (it was the early 1980s), and I figured that people would want to come to an upscale cowboy bar and eatery. It was only an intuition at the time, but I felt strongly enough about it to commit to creating a place that I knew people would love.

Starting construction

I also researched and found the big place in that genre at the time was Gilley's in Texas, and we drove there to get some idea of what to do. It was huge and well run. Food and all. They had a mechanical bull. I decided against that. I also grabbed a bunch of tumbleweeds from the Texas desert and brought them back with me for decorations.

There was another bar in Daphne called the Pecos Plantation. It had a mechanical bull. Competition never worried me, and I was right. Sometime later, after I opened my new venture, Rick's Place, Pecos Plantation closed down. I felt certain we were the cause of their closing.

Porch built and enclosed

The first thing I did after buying the Alamo was gut the place, and then built walls to enclose the outdoor porch to add more indoor square footage. I had other ideas as well.

The ten foot in diameter wagon wheel I had built

A friend and I built a custom ten-foot wagon wheel (with thirty-two pin-spots) that would be on the ceiling above the dance floor and hold the lighting. On the perimeter of the dance floor was big Fresnel lighting. I hired a big lighting company out of Los Angeles. I paid for them to come and I put them up in a motel in order for them to design the perfect lighting and sound system. The theme throughout would be urban cowboy – including the food. Steaks.

I was designing the place I wanted … no one telling me what

to do. That's the part I always loved the best. I could picture everything before it was built. It was exhilarating. The first time in my life I really got to create something I would be proud of. The construction took a lot of money, and the other aspects of the club did as well. But I was determined to make this the best it could be, without any shortcuts.

With porch enclosed

I even purchased a custom sound system that cost $18,000 (it would be $40,000

today) that would be used for live music, and then music between acts by a DJ on the opposite side of the dance floor and band. Non-stop entertainment. First class all the way.

Opening night was coming up, and we rushed to get it finished. The crowning achievement was the sign in the front:

Arcade with new enclosed porch

Rick's Place

The sign was of a huge Texas longhorn with my name below it. We even had an authentic wagon with wooden spoke wheels in front of the place. Everything was set.

The purchase of the building included ten acres of open field, which we allocated for parking. I was thinking big.

We were finally ready to open, and I put out the word with flyers and ads. A big crowd showed up on opening night. People had never seen anything like this, and they were impressed.

Eddie D at Rick's Place

Unfortunately, there was one big hitch. A family with their grandfather was at a table and asked their grandfather to dance with them. Finally, he relented, got up to dance, and dropped to the floor. My son, Brett, who played the guitar with the house band, said the man's face was blue.

What a terrible thing to happen to that family. And to us. A man dying in the middle of the dance floor on opening night.

The ambulance came and took him away. What a way to start my new venture. So sad. I hoped it wasn't a warning of things to come.

Word spread and pretty soon Rick's Place was the place to go. It got so busy in the evenings that the sheriffs had to direct traffic on 104 to get everybody in and out of the parking lot, as well as parking on both sides of 104.

Rick singing with in house band

Joe T., a big car dealer from Mobile, would come over all the time to eat. He would call and I would have my maintenance guy Acey meet his limo in the front and park it. Mayor Nix from Fairhope and others would come meet him, and they would eat dinner and then leave before the evening entertainment.

As I mentioned, we specialized in steaks; we had a cowboy and cowgirl T-Bone steak, which were both huge. We also served a pretty full menu with some seafood, but the emphasis was on steaks. People really liked them.

Back to the Future

Another friend showed up one night in a DeLorean automobile (like the one featured in the *Back to the Future* movie). It was new and beautiful. All stainless steel. He threw me the keys and said to take it for a drive. I did, and it drove as well as it looked.

When I returned with it, I went inside and told him how much I enjoyed the drive. He asked me for the keys. I said I left them in the car. Turns out, the door locks automatically when it closes. We had to break one of the rear windows to get into it.

I thought he would kill me, but he took it okay.

Rick's Place Prospers

In addition to making sure the food was the best in the area,

Rich Freeman at the DJ's booth

I focused my attention on making sure there was plenty of entertainment in the evenings for the bar crowd. I had a house band, and DJs would play music when the band took breaks.

I also would have talent contests on Tuesday nights with a $200 cash prize. Andy Andrews, the nationally known comedian, would try out his new routines and jokes on some of the Tuesdays, and if he won, he wouldn't take the money. But I made sure he was well fed.

I walked around each night making sure everything was going smoothly. Mable M. bought me a glass because every time I set mine down, I would forget where I left it. It was a glass with a chain that hung on my neck. It worked well. Every time I would order a drink, I would put a lime peel in the glass to keep track of my drinking.

Cup I wore around my neck to keep track of drinks – given to me by my bar manager Mabel

It didn't work, since I really didn't care. But the customers would laugh and loved to see how many lime peels were in the glass.

Halloween

Rick and Gari

I always liked Halloween, and especially dressing up in costumes. We came up with the idea to hold a Halloween costume contest at Rick's Place and we (and everyone else) would go all out to dress for the part. One year, I came in as the Lone Ranger – ON A HORSE! I rode it through the door and on to the dance floor, whooping and hollering, while the crowd yelled and clapped. I had gotten the horse from a neighbor named Leonard, and he saddled it up and had it ready to go. Gari came as a cowgirl. It was a good thing we couldn't win … or we would have.

One slight problem: the dance floor was so slick that the horse lost its footing, and its legs slid outward from underneath him. He did a spread eagle and ended up on his belly. The horse was able to get back up on all fours, and I rode him out with a hearty, "Hi-yo, Silver!"

The Set-Up

One night, I was approached by some semi-regular customers. They asked to speak with me, privately. We went into my office.

"Rick, we need your help," one of them said.

"Sure," I replied.

"Do you know anybody that has a barn we could … store some weed in overnight?"

"No, I don't know anybody."

"You sure?" they said. "We'll pay them $100,000 and take care of you, too."

I was sure. I didn't want to get involved with anything to do with pot. I told them that again. "I can't do it. Sorry."

They seemed to accept that and left. I was glad.

However…

Sometime later, some other people approached me with a different request.

"We have some money we need to put into an account. Do you have one we could use?"

I don't know why people would associate me with that kind of stuff. Maybe it's my name or the association with it.

What is this all about, I wondered? First of all, I didn't have a non-business account, and more importantly, I didn't want to do anything illegal. It would take a very naïve person not to feel this way. And they looked, well, like cops to me.

"No, I really don't," I said.

"We can pay you a nice commission for doing it," they continued.

I was adamant that I would not do it. We shook hands and they left.

The next day, police and federal agents swooped into the bar and arrested six of my customers, who, I am guessing, did take the bait they were offering.

That's My Finger

When people drink, which they did at Rick's Place, there were the occasional arguments that happen at any club. They were usually short lived and ended quietly. However, one night some customers got into a fight that escalated to where we had to call the police in to settle it.

One of the policemen was pointing a finger at one of the men, and the man grabbed his hand and bit off the finger. I couldn't believe it. Blood gushed, customers screamed, and the policeman was in shock. It did not end well for that customer.

Because of that incident, I hired a bouncer, a big guy who looked tough, and his showing up when arguments arose would usually solve the problem.

House Band

We had a house band with a blind piano player. His name was Eddy Delude, and he looked and sounded like Ronny Milsap. Once, he was sitting in a dune buggy outside the club. He must have accidentally hit one of the controls or something, because it took off and hit the restaurant's air conditioning unit.

Rick singing with blind keyboard player Eddie D in background

My son Brett was also in the band. They were really good. We had a female singer, Judy Best, who sang and sounded like Janis Joplin. When the band took breaks, we had a DJ on the opposite side of the dance floor on a twenty-foot platform and he would spin records until the band came back.

Rick's Place rocked all the time.

We were so busy, we had to open up a separate service bar to help service our customers.

Life was great. Business was great. I had finally found my niche. I was happy, making great money and everything looked up.

Then I went to New Orleans

The Phone Call That Changed It All

My mom, Grover, Gari and I were in New Orleans, getting away for the weekend, as we often did. I called Gari's sister Jackie from the hotel to check on the kids and things.

"Hi, Jackie, this is Rick. How is it going?"

"Fine, Rick."

"How are the kids?"

"Kids are fine … but … Rick's is gone."

"You're kidding. What do you mean 'Rick's is gone'?"

"It's burning down as we speak."

I thought about why she didn't call before then to tell me. I was numb.

"We'll be there just as soon as we can."

That ended our trip, and a large part of our livelihood. I was heartbroken, scared, wondering how bad it was. The drive back seemed to take twice as long as the first part.

Still Smoking

We pulled up and Rick's Place was still smoking. A pile of wet wood and ashes. It was the first time in many years I teared up; they flowed liberally down my cheeks. I searched through the rubble and found fifteen quarters, melted and in a pile.

I looked to Gari and we hugged. I was trying to reassure her we would get through this, but the truth is I didn't have a clue how we would. Rick's Place was the most successful enterprise I had ever created. And now it was gone. Just like that.

The big kick in the pants came later, when the insurance company paid me $20,000 for the loss. I was severely

Rick's Place - smoldering remains

underinsured. I made more than that in a week. And I had five times more than that in equipment in the club.

I at first suspected a competitor, H.G., who had a place called The Supper Club in Summerdale, had been responsible, because once we opened, we heard their business dropped tremendously. That was wrong of me to think that. The fire investigator told me it was an electrical fire that started in the rear of the club.

One point I'd like to make here. I always thought when I heard of people's businesses burning down that it was an owner's doing. Now my opinion has changed. I now understand how hurt you can get in a situation like this. I was totally wiped

Remains of Rick's Place

out. I am probably the only bar owner who had a fire burn up his club where the owner was NOT the cause of it.

I did hear a story, but I have no idea if it is true. The Fairhope fire department arrived about the same time as the Silverhill fire department did, but the police would not let them fight the fire. It was out of their jurisdiction, and they were told to hold off and let Silverhill handle it. It was said they could have saved the club. But it is hard for me to believe that could be true.

Now, I had to create a new business, and quickly. I took a breath and started thinking about what to do.

A Brief Interlude

Between Rick's Place and my next venture, I decided to go back to my roots in Lincoln Park and relax. And that meant playing some gigs. I took my son Brett and his friend Pete, a bass guitarist. We packed up and we drove up to Michigan. I had an old friend who had a club called The Bump Shop. Brett and I played there.

The owners of the Bump Shop had a son who owned a bar called Flappers. My room was upstairs directly above the jukebox. Turns out, every morning they had a cleaning lady come in around 6 am and clean the club. Only problem was, she turned on the jukebox full volume and played this one annoying song over and over (I won't mention which song here, out of respect for my readers).

Cousin Jimmy

While there, we ran into my cousin Jimmy Garrett. He was known as a kind of tough guy in Melvindale, Michigan. He was the son of my mother's sister, the one who recently died at 104 years old.

Jimmy came and visited us and we always went to this little diner next door after the club closed. We were sitting there one night, and some biker guys walked in. Jimmy stared at them. Jimmy had no fear.

As a side note, I remember one time, as a teenager, I went to a party that Jimmy invited me to. I was just a teenager and this guy started threatening me. Jimmy was in the other room and found out about it. He went in there where the guy was, hoisted the guy up the wall and told him he would kill him if he didn't keep his hands off his cousin.

Back to the story.

These bikers were tough looking. It was Detroit, after all. Jimmy looked up at them and said something like, "You guys look good in cheap clothes." I'm thinking *we're gonna get into a fight*, but they just nodded, turned away and kept moving. Jimmy wasn't massive in size, but he was muscular and had that aura that if you screwed with him, he'd beat the hell out of you. And he probably would.

Rick and Cousin Jimmy

In the restaurant business, you can't call the police every time. Sometimes you have to deal with it yourself. Several times, I've had to confront someone and my anger would come across as confidence and would make them give in, thinking maybe they shouldn't mess with this guy.

I've had guys back down from me when they had no business to. They would calm down and behave, when really they could have wiped the floor with me. But having no fear somehow evens the playing field and it has served me well in a few particular instances. I have learned that fighting accomplishes very little and usually leads to more serious problems.

We stayed in Detroit about a month and a half. During that period, I got to spend time with Brett and Pete, and we had a nice time together. We visited many of the old places where I used to sing. But I knew I had to get back and start to create a living.

We were running out of money.

Gulf Shores I

After my trip to Michigan, I was at a loss as to what I was going to do. Rick's demise was pretty well known all over because we were a very popular place. I had the reputation of being successful in the nightclub business.

That's when a lady contacted me. She had a place in Gulf Shores that had failed, and she wanted to see if I was interested in partnering with her.

I am purposely not naming her, so will refer to her as Cindy. I listened to her story, checked out the location, and after discussing it with Gari decided to open it with her as a silent partner. That's when Cindy's dad warned me not to let her handle any money. I found that a strange warning because they were wealthy people. Her mother was mayor of a city in Lower Alabama and worth millions. I didn't listen.

The restaurant had been closed down. It was named after her boyfriend and called Lambert's. Before that, it was Kenny Stabler's place – Lefty's. He was a former Alabama pro quarterback. It failed, too. So, they came in with Kenny Lambert (who was also a singer). That venture didn't make it either. That's when they approached me.

I made a deal – 50/50. She held the lease with the landlord. The deal was for the business only. It was located at Bayou Village in Gulf Shores.

First of all, I had to spend a lot of money, and I didn't have a lot to spend. Remember, I had only received $20,000 from the insurance proceeds from Rick's Place, and that was it.

I renamed Lambert's "Rick's", hoping to parlay the success of Rick's Place to that location.

Rick's became real big during that time. Right after Hurricane Frederic, timeshare sales were very popular and there were a lot of people from up north buying into them.

But they were an older crowd.

I created a sixteen-foot buffet with all kinds of food I gave away for free. I did this because I knew I would sell a lot of drinks. I did it in the motif of a 1950s diner and dance club. The waiters and waitresses were dressed accordingly. We played 50s music. People came in from about lunch to eight or nine in the evening, and then business suddenly dropped off.

I knew I had to change it to a younger group at night, like more of a Michael Jackson-type theme that was popular at the time. The club transitioned to a really nice place that catered to younger people from nine until about two in the morning.

I kept putting all the profits, which were substantial, in the bank.

The Money Deal

Two fellows came into Rick's all the time. They considered themselves big shots, spending money and flashing it around. I got the feeling that maybe they were sizing me up. For what, I had no idea.

Finally, they suggested that maybe I should consider opening up a Milo's-type hamburger place in Gulf Shores. It could be really successful. I told them I knew of the place and was interested in visiting the location in Birmingham. I'd heard their operation was great and they had a secret sauce for their burgers. They approached me with an interesting proposition.

"Rick, we'll fly you up on our airplane so you can visit Milo's and see their operation. We're going up there anyway and glad to help you." What a sucker I was.

I took my manager, Tom, and we flew up with them. We ended up at a house with some other fellow, and the conversation grew into whispers. They asked us to go upstairs while they finished the conversation. After that, we went to Milo's, and I did get a few ideas after peeking through the windows.

The two guys told us they were flying on to somewhere, but they had rented us a car and we could drive it to get home to Fairhope. However, they had something that needed to be delivered to a man in Montgomery and they needed us to deliver it. They gave us a location and a time to meet him. I guess they knew how long it should take to get there. They said the man was a retired FBI agent and would be standing on a corner. Which sounded weird to me, but we agreed anyway.

One of them handed me a leather-looking banking folder that was zipped up.

We drove from Birmingham to Montgomery. I kept looking at the bank bag and wondered what was in it. I was scared to open it, but curiosity got the better of me. Inside was over $35,000 in cash. Holy moly, what had I gotten into?

Tom was driving, and we got a bit turned around. This made us late. When we arrived, there was a man on the corner. He was pissed. In fact, he was so mad he couldn't even talk. I rolled down the window, gave him the package, and he angrily grabbed it, turned around and left.

We drove back to Fairhope and never saw those guys again. I guess they had sized me up ... for a sucker.

Almost as Good as Rick's Place?

Rick's was a great location, set on a huge elevated platform. The Original Oyster House was on the opposite end, with a couple of clothing stores between us. I created a great business there. We were busy even through the winter – in other words, we were doing really well.

We needed to have more liquor storage to keep up with our business. We ended up building a chicken wire storage shed to keep our liquor on the patio area. We had just got that built and were getting ready for the busy season in January.

However, problems were developing. The biggest was Cindy coming in with ten to twelve people at a time, eating free food and drinking, and not even tipping the waitresses. Finally, I told her to stop doing that. It put a big wall between us. She came from money and felt privileged. I was looking out for our profits.

We had been open for at least a year when the sh*t hit the fan.

Business with Friends

Before going on, I have to digress a little and mention something else that happened.

I had a buddy from the old days in Detroit who was basically a music groupie. He would come hear me sing and we became good friends. He was an architect by trade. Coincidentally, his wife was the girl I mentioned earlier who asked me to go steady in high school.

Gari and I had opened up a place called Papa Rocco's a few months after getting Rick's Place going. When I told my buddy, Bill, about Papa Rocco's, he asked if he could become part of the business.

It was a great location in Gulf Shores, and I had always wanted a pizza place since I missed out on the one in Fairhope. Gari was the driving force on this one. We bought the building, equipped it and copied Domino's Pizza for taste, back when Domino's Pizza was good.

We actually opened it as two restaurants at once. If you went in one door, it was pizza. You go in another door on the side,

Hwy. 59 & W. 6th St. — 968-PAPA

and it was oysters. It really worked out great. The pizza business was Papa Rocco's and the oyster business was Rocky Raw Shucks.

I named the pizza business after my father, whose name was Rocco.

When we first opened it, you had to walk up eleven feet of steps to get to it – a city ordinance because of hurricanes. Once we opened, they changed the height to seven feet, and we lowered the restaurant to seven feet, and that is when it really took off.

It had been open several months when my so-called good friend Bill proposed the idea of becoming part of the business. I wasn't keen on it.

I told him, "Business and friends don't work, I've never seen it work." He said he'd walk away before he'd let anything happen to us or our friendship. Boy, he got me real good.

Gari and Rick

The deal we made was for him to own thirty percent of the pizza and oyster business for $30,000. The money came in handy, and I thought it was more than a fair deal for him. He was a friend.

I had my attorney draw up the paperwork and we both signed. I didn't notice one particular part of the deal. I have a bad habit of not reading every line because I always assume the attorney knows what he is doing. However, Bill did notice and yet said nothing to me about it. How did I find out about my attorney screwing up big time?

I was not to learn about it until a little while later.

The Sh*t Hits the Fan

After Bill was running Papa Rocco's, he told me he wanted to get involved with everything I'd gotten involved with. I said, "Look, I'll get in touch with my partner Cindy and maybe she'll sell her half of Rick's to you, whatever you guys agree on."

It had nothing to do with me and I left it at that.

Every penny we made at Rick's went in the bank, in an account that you could subpoena and look at. So, as I said, that's when we added liquor storage on the deck for the winter. At that time, in the early 1980s, Gulf Shores wasn't popular in the winter at all and yet we were able to make money during that time going into our season. I felt good about that.

I gave Bill the contact info for Cindy and he called her.

Turns out that, to her, his phone call was a red flag, like I was pushing her out and stealing money, which wasn't the case. I didn't care either way if she sold or not. It was not a big deal in my mind. Apparently, it was a really big deal in hers.

After he approached her with the deal to buy her out, she sent her Gestapo guys and illegally closed us up while we were there working.

They came in and said, "We're closing the bar." Can you believe they could do that without even a court order? Or maybe they did have one, I don't know. But to close the bar and not have a legal reason? She sent policemen. Some in uniforms, some in plain clothes. Very official looking. And frightening, too. Her family was very powerful. When the police tell you to go, you go!

They said, "You gotta leave." My wife Gari and I left, and they locked it up.

I contacted my attorney and I found out later he's a damn friend of Cindy's. He tells me to just let her open the bar again, it's an ongoing business; when we come to a settlement, it'll be worth more if it is running successfully, and you'll get a better half. After all, we were 50/50 partners.

But her name was on the lease, and that is where I messed up. I should have paid her off, but I didn't have the money. I should have at least gotten my name on the lease with her. Without that, I had no power.

Cindy came back and opened it. Then I lost my attorney because … he was in her pocket. It created a conflict of interest, he sheepishly told me. I think he was scared of her and the power her family wielded.

Then I got a new attorney from Marion, Alabama. He came down and said it's cut and dry; you're in great shape, there is no way we can lose this case. He'd take the case and we'd win it. I never heard from him and kept trying to call him.

Finally, I did reach him. He told me on the phone, "If I take this any further, I'll never be able to practice law in Alabama."

Cindy and her family were that powerful.

In the end, I had nothing from all the work and money I had put into that venture. I was pretty near broke. Maybe it was karma, but the place failed a couple of months after Cindy reopened it. In spite of being the beginning of the season. However, she did get all the money from the bank account.

By the way, this Cindy was the same person who, when a funeral went by, would kneel at the curb and say a prayer. How phony could one be?

We were left with no money, a number of mortgages, and my "friend" Bill never contacted me. I got the distinct impression he was trying to avoid me.

After what I considered a royal screw-over from Cindy, I felt deflated. Depressed. I knew I was wronged, but that didn't change the fact that a successful business had been ripped from under my feet, and there seemed to be nothing I could do about it.

Attorney after attorney would not take the case, even though it was cut and dried; they said the family was too powerful to take on.

Most importantly, I had a family and five sons that I needed to support.

I should have gone over to Papa Rocco's and taken it over. I was seventy-percent owner. But I was numb and beaten down. I think I was still pissed off because I blamed Bill for the whole episode. If I hadn't let him in, he would not have approached Cindy, and I would still have had two restaurants. I also do not think she would have acted the way she did, but I could be wrong.

To this day, I wonder why I didn't take it over. But the truth was, I felt like I needed to prove something.

I had to decide what to do. And then a new opportunity presented itself.

Gulf Shores II - Easy Street

There was a real nice existing bar I was aware of in Gulf Shores called Easy Street. It was mainly a local businessman's bar that was not doing well. It was located out of the way in a commercial area. I approached the owners and suggested I take it over. They were happy to accommodate. They knew my reputation in the restaurant and bar business. I was sure I could make it work.

The owner of the building sent me to a banker friend of his named Bob and I told him my idea. He approved a signature loan of fifty thousand dollars, with no collateral. He sent me to the bank and five minutes later I had the money. I was surprised – shocked really – and also happy about that, because I then had working capital. Turns out, Bob and the owner were close friends and wanted me to be in the building.

I went about almost doubling the space of Easy Street and changed it from a small businessman's hangout to a local tourist destination. Based on the success of Rick's, I opened a free food bar during happy hour. My thoughts were that the sale of drinks would more than make up for the cost of food, like it did at

Rick's. I hadn't counted on one thing.

Snowbirds.

When news of the free food spread, they flocked to Easy Street, devouring the food and only ordering water.

Inside of Easy Street

Word about the free food got out quick.

All my local customers complained to me about the snowbirds. They had taken up all the seats and spent nothing. The locals had to wait in line behind the non-drinkers. After a

Cove Commercial Park
"Behind Southtrust Bank"

few months, I had to put a stop to the free food or risk losing the business altogether.

BILL HALEY'S COMETS

We still kept the happy hour but discontinued the food bar, which dropped the snowbird population almost immediately.

Easy Street was basically a bar with piano music, which I and others provided. I decided to mix it up and made Sunday night a special night with live music.

I contacted and hired a booking agency, telling them I wanted 1950s doo-wop groups. They brought a few: The Platters, The Diamonds, The Del Vikings; but they also brought some 1960s groups as well: Herman's Hermits, The Box Tops, and others.

I charged a cover charge at the door that paid for the group, and word got around quickly that Sunday night at Easy Street was the place to be in Gulf Shores.

One time, I hired the Chippendales to come in and barred all men (except for

The Platters

me, of course) from coming into the bar before 11 pm. The

women were going crazy, even stuffing money down my pants.

THE DIAMONDS

I'm sure a lot of husbands were thanking me later that night.

All this time, I was dealing with attorneys— the most prominent being a bankruptcy attorney named Finkbohner. Even though the new place was going well, and I was making money, debts were piling up. I had three houses with mortgages, and other debts as well.

My inward plans were to operate Easy Street while waiting to get to court and get Rick's back, but they kept delaying the court date with rescheduling.

I knew, if given enough time, I could work myself out of the debt. But I also had purchased the three houses in Gulf Shores when the money was flowing from Rick's that I was paying for,

my revenue had stopped from Rick's, and I wasn't getting any money from Papa Rocco's either.

But Finkbohner was not sure I could work myself out of debt and was telling me otherwise. He kept pushing us.

Herman's Hermits

Reckoning

"I'm afraid you'll have to file bankruptcy."

The words rang in my head like a tin drum. I remembered thinking on the drive over to Mobile on the Causeway that maybe there was another way. I was getting advice from a few friends, none of them attorneys, and the choices ranged from "tell everyone to (expletive) off," to what I was now hearing from a prominent bankruptcy attorney.

Bankruptcy.

My family and friends would have been horrified at the thought.

I was about forty-three years old, with five children, a great and supportive wife (thank God I had Gari, who was supportive through it all), a good home, and yet, here I was. What would I do after that? How would I be able to … to face everyone again? I'd been a singer, a successful restaurateur, and I was about to lose everything … even my family was at risk

"Mr. Gambino?"

"Yes?"

"Do you have any questions?"

"I do." I thought about what he said for a few more agonizing seconds. "Maybe we could, I dunno, work out payments to everyone … a payment plan."

"I'm afraid you have run out of options."

I guess he was right. The court case for Rick's never happened because attorney after attorney bailed on me.

He leaned forward on his desk, setting his arms on it and intertwining his fingers. "As I have said before, you have too much debt. If you file now, you'll be able to keep a few of your assets and get a fresh start. That's what you want, isn't it?"

A fresh start.

How many times had I already put my family through a fresh start? The moves. The traveling. The Christian years. The clubs and restaurants. I had thought we were finally through with all of that. I thought *Four successful restaurants and look where I'm at.*

"Mr. Gambino ... Rick?"

His voice drew me back to the present. "A fresh start sounds good. But to me, it's like giving up. And I never ..."

"It's not giving up, Mr. Gambino. It's giving you and your family a chance to start ... to start over. Create the life you want. That's the reason these laws are in place."

I just honestly felt he didn't think I was capable of starting over and doing another restaurant. It still sounded like giving up to me. Throwing in the towel. And I was not sure if I was ready to do that. I had been in some tough situations before and came through okay.

Nothing in my childhood upbringing had prepared me for this crisis. Although, my early years in Detroit's roughest neighborhood did teach me a thing or two about how to handle my future life experiences.

"Okay," I said, resigned. "Let's file the papers."

Opening menu for Gambino's

Menu for Rick's

Luke, Gari, Rick and Josh

Pile of melted quarters found in remains of Rick's Place

Rick at piano at Easy Street

PAPA-ROCCO'S   Pizza   968-PAPA

WHOLE PIZZA

	Reg.	Large
Cheese	4.85	6.95
Pepperoni	6.25	8.35
Sausage	6.85	8.95
Papa-Grande	7.30	9.60
your choice up to 5 items		

PIZZA BY THE SLICE

Cheese	1.15
Pepperoni	1.49
Sausage	1.59
Papa-Grande	1.59

Pasta

Baked Lasagna	2.99
Spaghetti & Meatballs	2.99
Spaghetti & Sausage	2.99
Spaghetti & Veal Parmigiana	2.99
Baked Ziti	2.99
Spaghetti Marinara	2.35

Calzones

Meatball & Ricotta	2.49
Spinach & Ricotta	2.49
Ricotta & Mozzarella	2.49
Sausage	2.49

Sub Sandwiches

Meatball Parmigiana	2.99
Veal Parmigiana	2.99
Sausage and Peppers	2.99

Salad Bar

2.25

With Meal	1.95
Under 12 Years Old	.99
Carry-Out	2.25

Beverages

	Reg.	Med.	Large
Pepsi			
Diet Pepsi			
Dr. Pepper	.50	.55	.65
Mountain Dew	Pitchers	2.25	
A & W Rootbeer			

Iced Tea	.40	Coffee	.29

DESSERT

Spumoni Ice Cream	.55

BEER & WINE

Michelob Draft

Premium	.85
Light	.85
Pitcher	3.79
Italian Red	.95
Italian White	.95
	By the glass

Add .25 To All Carry Out Orders

Papa Rocco's menu

Rick at the piano with Gari

Tommy Good and Rick

Even though we competed in Detroit we're still good friends

Never Give Up

Part Six

Betrayal and the Comeback
The Pasta Phoenix Rises

Bankruptcy

In the bankruptcy courtroom, I realized quickly that I had made a mistake. My so-called good buddy, friend for life, pal Bill, put himself on the list that he wanted Papa Rocco's for himself. And sure enough, the court awarded the pizza place to him – the entire business *and* real estate.

That was mainly because of the mistake my attorney made at the beginning, giving him thirty percent of the business AND real estate. So much for him walking away before hurting a friendship.

Bill just stood there, never looking at me, and quickly left after the hearing. I wanted to beat his ass, but didn't. It would have just multiplied my problems. Instead of coming to me and saying how can we work this out, he simply went along with the judge and, still to this day, operates the pizza restaurant that I named after my father. He closed the oyster side of the restaurant and made it a local party place – with bands and pizza.

Karma did catch up with him a little later.

I could not maintain Easy Street because I had filed bankruptcy and they took it back to cover the loan. It was a going business but did not generate enough cash flow to pay for everything. It definitely could have made it on its own. But I had no way to finance the operations of it with all the other debt.

I must mention here about Gari. She went along with everything and supported me like no woman could support anybody. It's amazing. Whenever I wanted to do something – move to Alabama, open a business, whatever – she was right there. If I had wanted to be a ditch digger, she would have stood right beside me and helped dig. And now she was supportive of the bankruptcy. I was truly blessed.

Still…

I had little left after the whole ordeal. I had no job, and really no prospects of a job. I don't, to this day, understand why I wasn't even more angry than I was. We lived in a rented house, and had no money coming in. And, because of the bankruptcy, I could not borrow any money from a bank.

There was some good news. I had purchased $5000 worth of Citizens Bank stock before all of that, on the recommendation of a friend, and I approached the landlord to see if they would accept it in lieu of rent for a little while. They agreed, and that gave us some breathing room. However, a few weeks later I watched out of our upstairs window as the bank repossessed our car from the driveway. Towed it away. I wondered if it could get any worse.

I bought an old, army-green, Pontiac Phoenix for $200 and resigned myself to starting over.

I approached Tony G., a manager at the Grand Hotel, about singing in the piano bar, which he readily agreed to. However, this was definitely the low point of my life. I had five sons, a wife, bills, was expected to make a living to support us all, and everything I had worked for up to that point in my life had been ripped away.

I remember coming out of a store, going to my $200 car on Fairhope Avenue, and seeing someone I knew. We were still a pretty big deal in the area because of Gambino's Restaurant. Very few people knew about the bankruptcy. So, instead of walking to my old beater of a car, I pretended to walk to another car as they watched me. I realized then I had hit as low as I cared to go.

Something had to be done … and right away.

The Grand Years

I dug in and sang my heart out every night at the Grand. It only paid $75 a night, but I made a good amount of money in tips. Enough to keep the family going. I would work until midnight and then go home. Gari didn't say much and was always there for me, whatever was next.

I tried to believe that things would work out and kept up my singing at the Grand Hotel for about three years. During this time (about 1986), Grover had completely run Gambino's Restaurant into the ground and finally leased it to a man named Ray T. who renamed it Palmer's. He tried to make a go of it, but was struggling, at best. Then, a seemingly unrelated business decision by Ray at the time turned out to be a wonderful opportunity for me.

He closed the bar side of the operation. Why? The air conditioner had broken, and he did not have the money to fix it. When I heard about this, my mind started churning and I came up with a plan.

Jolly's

I shared my idea with Gari, and she thought it might be a good idea and to give it a go. I approached Ray with a proposition.

"I would like to sublease the bar area from you," I said.

"You know the air conditioner is broken?" Ray said.

"Yes, but I will fix that as part of the deal. Also, I will pay half of the utilities and half the lease payment for the whole restaurant as part of the deal. In effect, you get half your utilities and rent paid, you'll have a bar open for your customers to order from, and it costs you nothing." He later put in a service bar to serve drinks to customers in his restaurant.

He liked the idea and we signed the deal. I had saved a little money over the previous three years so we could afford to have the A/C fixed, and then went to work fixing up the bar. We put in a little microwave and small convection oven behind the bar and added a pool table on a back-corner elevation. I planned on playing piano every night I could. I also had another idea. I wanted to name it after my grandfather, so we called it Jolly's.

Suddenly, I had hope again.

I continued playing at the Grand after we opened Jolly's, until we were making enough money for me to quit and sing full time at Jolly's. The customers moved to my new bar, and we were crowded every night. We stayed open late and got a lot of business from restaurant employees from around the area when they got off work.

Gambino's Rises from the Ashes

Grover had to finally run Ray off for non-payment of the lease at Palmer's. Even with us paying half the lease, the overhead was too much for him. Then Grover laid a bombshell on me.

"I am just going to open it up as Gambino's again," he said.

Oh, my God, I thought. I knew he couldn't do it. The last time he operated the restaurant was a disaster, and now he was planning on putting my name through the wringer again?

I told Gari about it and she was against us opening up Gambino's again. But I knew Grover would turn out terrible food and service and the customers would think it was us because it had our name. And besides, we would probably have to help operate it anyway. I decided to approach Grover.

"I have an idea. Let me lease the whole place and we'll open up Gambino's."

I secretly think this is what he had in mind all along. I leased it and started running both Jolly's and Gambino's.

Later, after operating Gambino's for a little while, I came up with another plan. I approached Grover again.

"How about you add to the lease that we get a first right of refusal to purchase the whole operation?" I asked. "But," I added, "I would like to set the purchase price in advance."

He said okay.

"But," he continued, "I still have a debt of $80,000. On the original mortgage. I can't sell it to you until it is paid off. You can lease it until it is paid off, then you can buy it."

We almost had instant success once Gambino's was up and running. When people heard we had the restaurant again, they flocked back and became loyal and supportive customers. After the restaurant was operating for a while, we really started to get back on our feet financially. And we still operated the bar section as Jolly's.

Life was getting better. The feelings I had from the bankruptcy were fading.

Gambino's lonely billboard on highway 98

Mine Again

A few years later, I wanted to initiate the purchase deal because Grover was not doing well health-wise, and I didn't want to have to deal with his daughter. When I told him I wanted to exercise the option to buy the place, he said the loan wasn't paid off.

I said, "I will pay off the loan and then buy you out."

He started having second thoughts but there was nothing he could do about it – it was there in black and white. We were doing well at Gambino's, and we somehow came up with the money to pay him.

Finally, Gambino's was mine once again.

During this same time, my dad let me know he was selling his house on Mobile Street in Fairhope, and that if I wanted it, he would sell it to me at the listing price and we would both save the sales commissions. He would even finance it for me.

I didn't know about that. I mentioned it to Gari, who thought it was a good idea. She wanted me to buy it. After some soul searching, I agreed, and my dad and I struck a deal. It was one of the best decisions of my life, and Gari was absolutely right about it.

During the next couple of years, I was refurbishing the nine little rental units I bought from my Dad and renting them out, which added tremendously to our income in addition to the restaurant's cash flow.

Trying to Make Nice...

Gari would always forgive everybody and anybody for anything. About a year after reopening Gambino's, she got hold of Rose, my "dear friend" Bill's wife, and said why don't you come to Gambino's and have dinner. If you remember, Bill is the good friend who ended up with Papa Rocco's Pizza free and clear after the bankruptcy. So, Bill, through this invitation, saw an opportunity to make good with me, kinda.

They came to Gambino's on a Friday night. We were packed out. Food and drinks flowing everywhere. I love that he saw that. I was playing piano and didn't get up; didn't socialize with them at all, although Gari did. In fact, I made a point of ignoring them completely.

Then, after we closed, Gari invited them to our home on Mobile Street. She brought them to the dining room table. I came in a few minutes later and they were sitting there, thinking we would have a good time, catching up or something. I just walked right by them and went to bed. Didn't say a word. My son Rich had to drive them back to Gambino's to get their car. That's the only other time I saw him since the bankruptcy. I didn't forgive so easily, and to tell the truth, still haven't. I need to work on things like that. The Bible says to forgive.

I was still thinking how he had left me in the lurch in the bankruptcy; literally stealing Papa Rocco's from me through the court system. Even though, as I mentioned earlier, he said he would walk away from the business before he'd hurt our friendship. Guess he forgot about that. And now, what? He wanted me to socialize with him again? I guess he thought all should be forgiven.

Don't think so.

One note of good news came a little later when Bill tried to open another Papa Rocco's in Robertsdale. Remember, I mentioned karma?

It went out of business in a short time. I know I shouldn't wish him ill will, but it shows it was my idea and Gari's idea – and the location – that made it work. And he didn't have our insight or abilities.

Secretly, I was happy about that particular failure.

I probably need to work on that, too.

Dad's Last Days

One evening, Dad complained of a pain in the back of his neck. I called an ambulance and they took him to Thomas Hospital. It was a Friday evening.

In the emergency room, they told me that there was no doctor on duty, and they would not be in until the following morning. They also said he looked stable and they thought it was indigestion or something to that effect. They agreed to keep him at the hospital until the doctor saw him the next morning.

Later, in the middle of the night, they called and said Dad had taken a turn for the worse, and I had better come there. When I arrived, they said he would not make it. I suggested they take him to Mobile Infirmary Hospital where they had a surgeon. But they thought he would not be able to take the ride over there and wouldn't make it.

"But if he stays here, you say he will die, yes?"

"Yes," they answered.

"So, what difference will it make if we try to get him to the Infirmary and take that small chance that he might make it?"

They couldn't answer that one, so we ordered an ambulance and took him across the bay to the Infirmary. I drove there and met him at the hospital. There were doctors on duty, and they took him into surgery right away.

I caught up with him as they were wheeling him into an elevator, and it was a horrific sight. His face was swollen to almost twice its normal size, and he looked scared. Without saying a word, I put my hand on his arm, smiled.

They were able to repair the main aorta, but there still was blow out damage on the artery near his abdomen, and they had

Rick's Dad

hoped it would clot on its own. They said they could not fix both at the same time They were hoping that blow out would clot.

They also said there was a ninety-percent chance of him not making it, in any event. He died shortly after the surgery. The second artery never clogged.

I was angry at the whole process at Thomas Hospital. I feel if a doctor had been on duty, he would have diagnosed it correctly and my dad would have had a fighting chance. How can a hospital have an emergency room without a doctor anyway? It is ridiculous.

Serena missed her dad terribly and lived with her mother for many years. Later, she moved in with me and I have taken care of her until recently, when she moved into her house with my younger brother, Mark.

My Mother's Last Days

My mother was a great lady. She was very talented. She could sing, play the piano and was tremendous at writing poems.

She also never seemed to lose her zest for intimacy with the opposite sex.

I remember when she was either in her late 70s or early 80s that she was staying in one of our apartments. An elderly, classy sort of man seemed interested and came to take her out. All I remember is him walking out of the apartment and my mom, a bit behind him, telling me she thought he was impotent.

Rick's Mom

TMI, Mom.

My aunt Marion, who recently died at 104, told me she thought my mom was the smartest of all the sisters.

My mom published some of her poems, and I cherish having a copy of that.

I posted a copy of her poems on the website.

She died at 84 years old of heart failure. I honestly think it was her taking a medication for the previous twenty years that was the real cause of it.

She had both side-effect symptoms the drug warned about.

I still miss them both all the time.

Rock Creek

Back home in Fairhope, I had thought from the time they had developed the project that Rock Creek was a well-planned and managed community. We were making a lot of money from Gambino's and I decided to have a custom-built home created

Interior of Rock Creek House

on the eighteenth fairway in Rock Creek. We bought a lot and started making plans for the dream house we always wanted.

The plans called for a total of 4000 square feet and had four bedrooms and a beautiful window overlooking the eighteenth fairway of the golf course. We also planned a pool in the back.

When there were groups playing on the golf course, like the Elks or Gambino's tournaments, I would put out a keg of beer and they could get a cup when they went by.

Once they started construction, problems started. I noticed a number of things were not right. Like windows not square, doorways crooked, wrong dimensions, stuff like that.

The builder was installing the trusses wrong, and he blamed the truss company. The truss company came out and measured everything, then came back and confirmed they were right, their measurements were correct.

What happened, briefly, was that Arthur Runtenberg built the prettiest houses in Florida. Builders would buy franchise areas. But this builder was screwing up so bad he had a lot of lawsuits. He wanted to get out of Alabama; in fact, he was rushing to get out of Alabama.

He used a builder to build my home who had only built cookie cutter homes – but the house I had designed for me was completely custom.

The supervisor would never show up. When the carpenters ran out of nails, I often had to run to the hardware store to get supplies and nails.

He was putting the trusses in the wrong place. Even I could see that. I could also see that the door openings were crooked.

Nothing was square or plumbed. It was a mess and very discouraging. So, I complained.

Finished house

When the builder was confronted, that's when he said he was right and the trusses were wrong; and the truss company came out, spent an entire day measuring and confirmed the trusses were indeed right. He quit before he could be fired.

We were going to Branson, Missouri, for a week and I didn't want to leave with all of the mistakes that were being made. I got my four-foot level, a tape measure, and a felt pen, and marked all the studs, showing the crooked door openings and other areas that were not level. It was a mess.

Kenny B., the new builder, said he would take care of it. When we got home, it was perfect.

I kept thinking how terrible it would be to spend $100,000.00 on a house lot and have everything crooked and out of plumb. With Kenny, the disaster finally ended. It didn't hurt that I brought the new crew lunch every day, and of course, a twelve-pack of beer when they got off at night.

The house was completed in about a year and we moved in.

I wanted a pool, but with a custom design. So, I took a stick and drew an outline on the ground and it accidentally looked like the outline to Mickey Mouse's head, with a hot tub between his ears. The builders liked my design so much they offered it to other owners, and it became very popular.

Hot tub in Rock Creek

We were making a lot of money every month, we had a beautiful home on Rock Creek, and I finally felt I could relax a little and start enjoying the fruits of my labor.

By the way, one time I was walking around the pool, in a suit, and tripped on the cement and fell into the pool. It was the only time I was ever in it.

The First One

After I built my house in Rock Creek, I decided to get a street-legal golf cart, and purchased it. I went to the city and asked them to license it. They had no idea what to do. They had never licensed a street-legal golf cart. They

didn't have a category for a golf cart. The carts were not in the system and they said it could not be licensed.

Here is what I did …

Because it was street legal as far as having headlights, windshield wipers, etc., I was pretty confident that it could be licensed. I didn't know if it had a VIN number, but they didn't have a category to put it in anyway. I insisted, and they finally made a decision and put it under dune buggies. And they gave me a license plate and made it legal. It was in the local newspapers.

It was the first golf cart ever licensed in Alabama.

Now they have a cart classification where you do need a VIN number in order to get it licensed.

Free Room and Board

Gari and I traveled to Michigan to visit our friends there. We had parties the whole time we were there.

At one particular one, we were drinking and having such a good time (me drinking more than I should have) that I invited all of my friends to come and visit me, free room and board. I would take care of everything except the airfare.

I was playing the big shot. There were ten couples. We had all grown up together and were lifelong friends.

Gari said to me later, "Do you realize what you just did? You invited them to come visit us for free. How are we going to do that?"

"They won't remember it," I said. "They were all drunk. You'll see."

The next day, they all asked when they could come down and said how much they were looking forward to it. I looked at Gari. Yikes.

I ended up paying some of my tenants to go on vacation and we were able to accommodate everyone. Tight, but comfy.

Party at Rock Creek

While we were all in Fairhope, a few went out shopping and sightseeing, with all twenty of us agreeing to meet and have a

The surprise party

cookout at my home in Rock Creek. We brought in a bartender and a small combo, including my son Brett from Gambino's.

When we walked in the door, the place was packed with friends and family. They yelled "Happy Anniversary!" Took us totally by surprise.

They gave me a tuxedo printed on a t-shirt, and they had a pretty hat and bouquet of flowers for Gari. It turned out to be a very special anniversary.

We had a great visit with them, but I never offered to do that again.

Up the Off Ramp

Before going on, I remember something else that happened I wanted to share.

I was in Michigan visiting my uncle Rich, when one of my best buddies, Mike C., invited me to his house in Wyandotte. We were partying in the basement where he had a little bar, meeting with all my school friends. My uncle came with me but left early, because he didn't really know anybody there. I guess he brought his own car.

The party went into the early morning. We quit around 2 or 3 am. I started to leave and Mike said, "Rick, you've been drinking, stay here."

But I was stubborn. I left and was in my car, going to find the motel where I was staying … maybe 20 minutes away. Of course, being so late (or early in the morning) there was no traffic. The problem was, I was not sure where my motel was located.

I finally saw it in the distance, on the left. I admit I had over-drunk a bit, and I saw this ramp that went up and toward the motel and decided to take it. I thought it would get me there. I started to drive up it and realized I was wrong. I was going up the offramp.

Then, behind me a police cruiser put his flashing lights on and stayed at the end of the offramp. Luckily, there was no one around and I put it in reverse and started slowly backing up toward him, realizing I had made a mistake

The policeman waited for me to back down the offramp. I'm guessing he didn't want to make the situation worse with two cars going up the offramp.

I stopped a bit in front of his car and immediately jumped out of my car and ran to the police cruiser.

He rolled the window down.

"Look, officer, I am sorry," I said. "I'm from Alabama, and I thought this was the way to get to the motel." I pointed to it over in the distance."

He was silent for what seemed like five minutes. I suppose he was thinking "Do I want to take this guy in?" He obviously knew I'd been drinking. Who else would be going up the offramp at three am if they were not drinking? He didn't say anything.

Finally, he spoke, pointing to another road. "Take that road over there. It will get you to your motel."

"Thank you, officer, I really appreciate it."

I got to the motel room, still a little dizzy, but thankful for the officer's kindness.

The next morning, I woke up and couldn't believe what happened, and thanked the Lord for not letting me get arrested the previous night. I think I promised God I wouldn't do that again … at least for a while.

I definitely deserved to be arrested.

I decided to drink only moderately from then on.

Commercials

Having a little more time on my hands with the restaurant going so well, I had a crazy idea. I don't know if it was collective between me and Brett, or if I was just going off the rails. We were both on the same level of insanity. But we decided we'd make a couple of commercials.

Catching a fish for commercial

We didn't want normal commercials – someone bragging about the business. So, we came up with a couple of novel ideas.

For the first one, we went out behind the restaurant to a fence that was no higher than my head. Brett was behind the fence on a ladder. We planned it out. I started out talking about spaghetti, and they threw spaghetti on me. Then seafood, and I caught a big fish Brett dropped. I mentioned chicken and a live chicken hit me on the chest. And finally, I mentioned our fresh garden salad and homemade dressing, which rained down on my head. ." Then bread pudding placed on my head and finished with hot raison bourbon sauce.

I was a mess, covered with food. My son Luke said, "Come on, Dad, clean up and let's do it again

Brett added the jingle and sound effects after we shot it.

Commercial two was different. That was across the street at the American Legion, between the road and the water. The idea was to tie the restaurant in to golf … Italian food being the key.

It showed Gari setting up to swing at a ball – only it was a meatball in a dish of spaghetti. She swings and hits the meatball and spaghetti, we hear her say "fore", and I turn back to look. The spaghetti and meatball hit me in the face.

I received different responses from different people. Most of our customers were great about it. However, one lady who came in told us it was ridiculous because you don't throw food. I don't know if she stopped coming in or not. I do know it would have been difficult to send that food we threw away to China.

Spaghetti all over me

On the whole, people loved the commercials, and they accomplished what we set out to do: bring in new customers and have people remember our restaurant. Again, Brett filled in sound effects and a jingle.

We played them on regular TV.

The Magic Trick...

Jerry Jones, owner of the Dallas Cowboys, and all his coaches came in every year when the senior bowl was being played. Regulars. I got to know him. He was a standup guy. He came in with all his coaches and Campo would sing karaoke.

One night, after a few drinks, and they were staying late talking football in the dining room, Jerry came up with an idea.

He was going to pull the napkin out from underneath the glasses. As he was bragging about how he could do it, without breaking the glasses, he pulled the napkin and everything hit the floor, glasses and all. What he forgot was the napkin had a sewn-in seam that probably made it impossible to perform that trick. But, as I said, drinks were involved.

Me and Josh with Jerry Jones and his Super Bowl ring.

I immediately waved to a busboy to clean up the mess, but Jerry waved him off.

Jerry Jones and crew

"It's my mess, I did this, and I'll clean it up." And he did just that.

Like I said he was a stand-up guy, and this just confirmed to me why he was so successful.

He was almost opposite from what I had heard and read about him. A true gentleman.

Down the Road and the Fish House

We always had a wait at Gambino's. We bought what is now Wintzell's and opened it as an overflow restaurant that we called Down The Road. We suggested to customers that instead of waiting two hours, they could go to Down The Road. It didn't work. People wanted to wait at Gambino's.

Building we purchased

We renamed it The Fish House.

It was a sports bar and restaurant. Thirty TVs and a couple

of big screens. On each table was a remote, where you could pick the screen you liked and listen to the audio on the device at the table. Plus, they had access to Trivia, which was very popular then.

In one of the rooms, the acoustics were too loud, so I draped flags from all over the world on the ceiling to help with the noise. We were very successful. However, managing two restaurants was becoming too much.

A few years later we sold the restaurant to Wintzell's.

The Fish House and the Commercial

The fish house grew into an idea when we realized people would rather wait an hour to eat at Gambino's than truck on down the road to eat at... Down the Road. We decided to create a great seafood restaurant and also a unique dining experience.

We put thirty television around the room and then supplied small remotes and speakers at each table where people could decide on what they wanted to watch and could listen to it at the table.

The commercial was Brett's idea, and it worked.

Inside Fish House with TV Screens

246

Brett created a goofy costume, wearing fins and a mask. He came out of the bay with a fresh fish. The camera follows him walking to The Fish House and walking in the door. The slogan?

'Where our fish is fresh.'

TV Show

Mediacom had a studio and a public access channel that was open to all Mediacom customers. Channel 27 on the dial. We decided to do a show, loosely based on *The Tonight Show* with Johnny Carson.

One of the first sketches we did was Brett being a gay chef from New Orleans and telling us how he invented a new sandwich – Pene ala butar… which in fact was peanut butter and jelly.

We did a man-about-town segment, with me interviewing people.

I did an opening monologue, and we hosted the whole show in one of our rental houses. We bought a huge mural of New York City. Built window frames around it and it looked like a real set. It only ran for eight weeks.

Why?

Because, as I explain in the next section, I sold Gambino's and decided to stop production. And besides, it was really time consuming. Brett would spend the night editing.

I did enjoy doing it, though. One time, I was walking in Fairhope and I heard this little boy say, "Mom, that's the man on television."

Oh boy, a fan.

All of these commercials and shows can be viewed on the website.

Gambino's Sold Again

As you have probably figured out about me by this point, I was never one to stay into anything for a long time. I always thought of creating new restaurants, and then I thought about selling when things were peaking and doing so well. Perfect time to get out.

But this time I had a different plan. I was only going to sell the business, not the land, building or equipment. This was a critical distinction that saved my ass in the future.

Sunbelt Business Brokers listed the property, and they found the buyer. The buyer, a fellow named Scott, finally came to my house in Rock Creek. He was impressed. He looked around and said "Man, you can afford a house this nice all from your restaurant?" This convinced him even more that the restaurant was a good deal … which it was.

He paid $920,000; $650,000 down. I held a note for the rest and had another note for the equipment.

Scott kept the name Gambino's, since that was all I was selling in addition to the equipment. He lasted three years. The problem was, he was running it from New Orleans, and he had no idea what was going on. He left his wife at the restaurant most of the time. She was nice, but in over her head.

One of the managers at Gambino's was a friend of mine. He told me Scott was closing up the place the following weekend. I hurried in and was in the process of changing the locks when he showed up. He was a big guy. Fuming. I thought he was going to kill me. I was a bit nervous, but I wasn't afraid of him. I was in the right.

I told him he was in default. I also mentioned someone told me that he was leaving that weekend, so I had to protect my assets. "You are in default of the lease, and you are not entitled to anything," I told him.

He stomped off, got into his car, and raced off.

Last time I ever saw him.

Gambino's Sold Again ... and Again

I went back to the Sunbelt brokerage company and they found another buyer. Scott had taken my name down pretty badly with shoddy service and food. I had to lower the price and had it for sale for $250,000.

A new buyer from Tulsa was found. He seemed promising. My two sons stayed to help him, and he ended up firing them both. He spent some money on it, yet went out of business in two years.

Turned out firing my sons was a big mistake. Without them he was doomed.

I then leased it for $8,000 per month triple net lease and thought I was through with it.

I wasn't.

San Diego

Another brief interlude. Gari and I decided to take a trip when all of this was going on to San Diego. One of the things we wanted to do was go deep sea fishing, so we took a boat that would go out to sea 150 miles to where the big fish were. This particular trip, you slept on the way out, and then you would wake up, have breakfast and fish. Every time I got up, I threw up over the rail. I was in bed the whole trip. Gari did some fishing, but every time I tried to get up, I was sick. I felt okay lying down.

Once back on land, we tried to get a room for the night but every hotel we went to was full. I was getting impatient because I was still dizzy from the boat. We stopped at each motel, and were elated to finally find one that had only one room available.

"Only one thing," the desk clerk said. "It has a waterbed."

I asked to see it, walked in and pushed a couple of times, looked at Gari and said, "I'm still feeling bad. I'm getting dizzy just pushing on this."

We continued on until, later that night, we found somewhere to sleep.

Gambino's... Yet Again...

One of the potential tenants I found wanted to enclose the patio. It faced west onto Section Street, and it was used for outdoor dining, weather permitting. But a good part of the year, it was unusable due to heat or rain. They insisted they wouldn't lease Gambino's until they got approval to enclose it.

I went to the city to apply for a permit and started the process. However, the city did not want to grant a permit because it would add to the parking issue.

Exasperated, I went back to the city and asked for their help. I told them it was bad for the city image-wise to have the restaurant closed on such a busy street, and although I had a tenant to lease it, they wanted it only if the deck could be enclosed. Plus, I reminded them of all the revenues from sales tax the restaurant would generate for the city, not to mention the employment.

Construction of deck begins

They called the building department and asked them if they could see their way to making sure that my patio enclosure went through.

Amazingly, permits appeared and the tenant was able to complete it.

I Have Had It

Still, the tenant defaulted a few years later.

By that time, I'd had enough of the buy/take-back game. I decided to find a class A tenant and lease it to them and be done with it. I was approached by Baumhauer to lease the restaurant, and then by Another Broken Egg … both potentially great tenants.

Another Broken Egg wanted the place for twenty-five years at a flat rate of $5,000 per month – not even triple net. I thought about it long and hard. It was a bird in the hand, and I would still own the building and property.

But the downside, and it was substantial, was that I would be on the hook for any repairs that were needed over those twenty-five years. It would be a potential disaster for me. I declined the offer. The lease would outlive me. Thank was a thank God move.

With that deal, I would pretty much be giving the restaurant away. I couldn't touch the real estate in my lifetime and would still be responsible for all repairs, including the roof, air conditioning and other maintenance. And, they wanted me to pay the taxes. At $5,000 per month, I would be at least $3,000 short of whatever the going rate was for an 8000 square foot restaurant, including the fully equipped kitchen and bar.

Then my second youngest son Josh approached me.

A Third Time?

"Dad," he said, "let's just re-open Gambino's. We can do it."

"Josh, I need to talk to one more potential lessee."

Baumhauer was interested and I felt I owed them a chance to make an offer. A few days later, they pulled out. I called Josh. "Okay, Josh, let's do it."

"That's great, Dad. You won't regret it."

I wondered: "How many comebacks can a person make?" That was the re-start of Gambino's, and I could not have done it without Josh. Over the years, he had managed a number of food businesses and was a great cook. Plus, he knew the business and I could trust him.

Even if he was not my son, he would have been my first choice to run the restaurant. He is that good.

A sweet deal for everyone.

Rising Again

Gambino's reopened in 2013.

Once word got around that the original owners of Gambino's were back, customers flocked to the restaurant like moths to a flame. We pulled out all the stops and thought how we could deliver the most value to our customers while maintaining the quality they came to expect. I know this sounds like a commercial, but the truth is we always think this way. It is, in large part, the backbone of why people like to come to Gambino's. I always ran the restaurant from the customer's chair.

Some of the awards we have won since we reopened are:

- Best Italian Restaurant in Mobile and Baldwin Counties.
- Top 200 restaurants in America.
- Best steak in Alabama that is not a steakhouse.
- Number one on Trip Advisor (Urban Spoon).

- And many more….

I am proud of these achievements. I had then come full circle from the first purchase in 1976 to finally opening it up with Josh running it the way we wanted. Life has a funny way of working out that way. And a roundabout way of getting you to your dreams. I could have done without many of the detours, but in the end, we were fine and now all we had to look forward to was the future, with none of the past holding us back.

I was working every day in Gambino's with my son Josh. My son Rich was in Mobile with a successful pizza restaurant called Delphina's; my son Brett is a top sales rep and sells us our food through PFG Performance Foods; my son Adam sells us our restaurant equipment with Mobile Fixtures and Equipment; and my youngest son Luke is a successful attorney, whose advice is priceless. He is also vice-President and general counsel of Coca Cola southeast.

As George Peppard used to say on the *A-Team*, "I love it when a plan works."

Shux

I had always felt that the Yardarm restaurant was a great location. A pivotal landing spot in town, on the water, but it needed a lot of work. It was tired, there was no deck, no bar, and it was strictly a place that served sea food. They did a nice job, but it was not being fully utilized

The owner and his mom put it up for sale. I made an offer for the full list price. Another offer came in at just under the list price. The real estate agent came back to me and said, "I have another offer, so I think you should both be able to bid up the price."

I said "Look, I am offering list price. Exactly what you asked for. Why should I continue bidding it higher?" And, truth be told, it kinda pissed me off that he wanted to turn it into an auction. "I don't think that is very ethical," I told him. He came back and said, "You're right. You offered the list price and you have the restaurant."

I went to the city and it was no problem to get it transferred. I already had a big restaurant in Fairhope, they knew me and my business ethics, so it was no problem to get it transferred.

We converted the porch into a bar, and put in the deck, which turned out to be the first place everyone wanted to sit. Outside and looking over the water. We had to redo the electricity, new plumbing, and a host of other issues. For instance, the sewer pipes had to be replaced. It took over six months to open but the effort was worth it. My cousin Sam Gambino made the logo for Shux. He is a great artist. In fact, he did the artwork for the cover of this book.

We opened and the public supported the restaurant right away. We were unique in the sense we shucked oysters behind the bar. We were an oyster bar and seafood restaurant, on the water, and in Fairhope.

It was exactly what I had envisioned for the place.

Closing Shucks

Shucking oysters is a great business to draw people in, but it is a terribly high employee expense and a mess. After a couple

of years, I decided we had to change the type of restaurant we were operating. Although it made money, the employee costs were too much.

I also wanted to add a gift shop to the front for all the tourists who came to the pier, and change up the menu a bit – offering more lunch and dinner items and some casual foods that were not just seafood. It became obvious we needed to change the name, too.

We picked The Pier for the name, since … it was on the pier. My cousin came up with a great logo with a pelican.

We're still operating and doing a good business.

Desperados Rick and close friend Mike

WEDNESDAY, AUGUST 30, 2000   BALDWIN REGISTER

RESTAURANT OPENING

Eastern Shore Chamber of Commerce representatives were on hand for the grand opening of Gambino's Down the Road in Fairhope. In attendance at the ceremony were, from left: front row, from left, manager Brett Gambino, owners Rick and Gari Gambino, manager Adam Gambino, chamber ambassador Sandy Cooke; middle row, chamber ambassadors Sue White and Denise Weston; back row, chamber ambassadors Kitty Bradshaw, Miriam Bailey, Dennis Sherrin and Kevin Wilson. Gambino's Down the Road is located at 860 S. Mobile Ave. For business hours or for more information, call 929-2322.

Four generations of Gambinos

Left to Right: Mike, Marge, Rick and Gari

Former Gambino's owner dies, services held Friday

By Ed Brock
Staff Writer

A prominent Fairhope businessman is dead at age 80 after 17 years as owner of one of the town's best known restaurants.

Grover Moss Johnson Jr., former owner of Gambino's restaurant on Scenic Highway 98 in Fairhope, died July 1 of stomach cancer.

Johnson was a Mobile native and graduate of Murphy High School in Mobile who lived for some time in Ridgewood, N.J., where he sold aluminum siding.

Johnson also owned a hardware store, but Gambino's current owner Richard Gambino said Johnson was happiest in the restaurant business.

"He was the feistiest, most energetic fighter you've ever seen," said Gambino. "He never quit. He got a lot out of life."

Gambino, who started the restaurant with his wife in 1976, said Johnson bought a minor interest in the eatery in 1978.

In 1980, Gambino said they sold the restaurant to Johnson and started another in Gulf Shores.

Johnson kept the name Gambino's until 1981, and then leased the building out under the name Palmer's. In 1987, the Gambinos returned and operated the busi-

Grover Moss Johnson Jr.

ness under Johnson's ownership until about two years ago, when the Gambino's bought the restaurant back.

Johnson was buried Friday at Magnolia Cemetery after a service at St. John's Episcopal Church on Government Street in Mobile. He is survived by his daughter and son-in-law, Laurel and Thomas Holland, and four grandchildren, Johanna, John, James and Joellyn Holland of Massachusetts.

Johnson's wife, Olive Martin Johnson, died in 1970.

Johnson was also an active member of the Crewe of Columbus and Le Krewe de Bienville.

Picture I drew of Grover

urbanspoon

03/20/13

Gambino's Italian Grill
18 Laurel Ave
Fairhope, AL 36532

Congratulations Gambino's Italian Grill!

Your restaurant was selected as one of the **Top 200 Most Popular Restaurant – Bars** on Urbanspoon in America this year. Urbanspoon users think you have one of the best places to grab a cocktail or a pint in the country!

Urbanspoon is the only social network dedicated to restaurants, food lovers, bloggers and professional food critics who share their dining experiences and pictures in one awesome place. With 1,000,000+ restaurants pages and 30,000,000 visitors monthly, Urbanspoon's website and mobile app are the most popular dining resources for finding the best restaurants in your city.

Named one of Top 200
Restaurants by Urban Spoon

Never Give Up

Part Seven

Past Successes and the Golden Years

Off, Off, Off Broadway

Part of the fun of owning Gambino's was always wanting to do something that would draw attention to the restaurant and bring in business; so, I would come up with a host of ideas – game shows, talent contest, things like that.

In the 1970s, after opening Gambino's, a friend and employee, Steve, introduced me to Gretchen Riggs. She was a retired theater producer. I thought we could do a dinner theater in our dining room. I suggested it and everyone thought it was a good idea.

We began to build a set. As you may have already guessed, I never wanted to do anything halfway, so we built a first-class backstage area. It took up half of our dining room. We had it so everything could come from behind the stage, making it look as professional as possible.

The show was called "Dirty Work at the Crossroads". It went over like gangbusters. People loved it so much, we decided to do another one. I asked the producer if I could get a small bit-part in it. They ended up giving me the lead in a play called "Charlies Aunt". It also was a great success. I loved doing it.

The plays were sold out both times. I have a picture of me in costume during the show and also a copy of the program, both posted in the lobby of Gambino's.

We ended up stopping the dinner theater because we only got one turn of the tables with only half the dining room. Successful restaurants need to do two and a half turns per evening. We took down the stage and went back to normal business and were left with only fond memories of that time. And, we continued to do great business.

Games at Gambino's

We had a lot of game shows at Gambino's, in the bar area. We had a gong show that was so popular, we would fill the room every Wednesday with standing room only. It was a hoot. It took all week to convince people with guts enough to do it because they knew they would probably get gonged. But in the end, everyone had a good time.

My son Brett did the Unknown Comic. He was hilarious, and the whole concept became so popular that when the dining area closed, we had to move it the stage over to that area to accommodate all the people.

We had a banana eating contest that was ... well ... special. We would get one of the employees from the back, usually one a little slow, and then two other "volunteers". We would put them on stage, blindfold them and set the bananas in front. The one who ate the most would win.

What we didn't tell the set-up guy was when we said to start, the other two guys just sat back, and only the one who was the set-up guy was eating the bananas. The poor guy would shove the whole banana into his mouth beyond capacity and choke continually. The crowd roared with laughter.

One time, the set-up person came to me and said he heard that he was the only one eating the bananas. I told him that was nonsense and that all three were. He said okay and went back to work.

One of the things we did was advertise a beer drinking contest. Surprisingly, we had a lot of volunteers for that. What we didn't tell them was that they would be drinking the beer from a baby bottle – with bonnets on their heads. We had a lot of fun.

A couple of times, I followed women into the restroom with a cordless mic and started interviewing them. They were good-natured about it and the audience loved it.

The Dating Game

This was a favorite of mine, because it really got the crowd involved and usually had a happy ending. We would get six people – three men and three women (we would always try to get nice-looking contestants – men and women), and they would sit on either side of a screen so they could not see each other. We would ask questions a little racier than the TV show, and the crowd loved it.

When we finally had a winning couple, I had a friend with a boat who would take them on a romantic cruise around Mobile Bay, and then they would get a nice dinner at Gambino's to top off the date night.

We also had great singing contests, Halloween parties, costume contests and much more.

Great fun, and I loved emceeing everything we did.

Vacation Home

During this time, I decided to buy a house on Lake Erie, but technically it was on the Detroit River which is part of Lake Erie. The summers were brutal here in the South, and I wanted a place to go and visit the many friends I grew up with and also take the family where we could enjoy the weather and be by water.

I paid $360,000 for the house. It was a beautiful home right on the water. I put on a large deck and remodeled the house extensively. There wasn't a better view anywhere, and we used

Vacation home in Grosse Ile

it as often as we could. At first.

There were sailboat regattas and you could look east and literally be seeing Canada. In a word, it was a lovely location.

I didn't want to lease it out, because I wanted it available for my family. After a couple of years, it started to become a financial drain. We weren't using it as much as I had hoped. This was in 2009, when the

House with deck Rick Built

market started tanking. I finally decided to sell it and lost over $150,000 on the deal. Sold it for $300,000. So much for real estate outside of Fairhope, although we took a hit here, too. But not nearly as hard as we did in Michigan.

On a Trip with the Gang

One of the themes I've tried to show is how much I value friendships. I have had friends from the old neighborhood since I was a little kid, and we've kept up those friendships over the years.

The gang – lifelong friends

Many times, we would take trips together. One of the most memorable was going to a river in Tennessee, where we rented a houseboat, and all stayed on it.

Great friends and great fun.

My Run for Mayor

I was approached by a friend in the building industry who asked me if I would consider running since we had heard Mayor

Tim Kant was not going to run. I liked Tim and considered him a friend (and still do). This friend said he could get the homebuilders to support me and would create a PAC to fund the campaign.

Why not? I thought.

And that was the start of it. I had flyers and business cards made and started my campaign in full swing. Problem was there

were a few other people who also were running. And I might point out this was during the time Gambino's was not in operation and hadn't been for a few years. In other words, my name hadn't been in the public for a long time.

All was going well until I found out the homebuilders were suddenly backing another candidate, much to my surprise. Okay, I can deal with that, I thought.

However, the real surprise came when one of the candidates invited me to his home and shared with me how he thought I should drop out of the race – he felt he was the only one who could beat Tim Kant. This pissed me off. I suggested that maybe he should drop out so that I could beat him. Needless to say, neither one of us dropped out and neither one of us beat Tim Kant either.

Such is politics.

Where Did it Come From?

Gari and I were in Gulf Shores at the convention center having lunch. It is a big concrete building right by the water. We had a very country looking waitress who came to take our order.

"What'r y'all having today?"

"The clam chowder," I said. Then I asked, "Is it Manhattan or New England?"

She thought for a moment. "I think it's Campbell's."

It's a What?

Lastly for this section, Franco S. opened up an Italian Restaurant in Mobile called La Louisiana. We loved the place and would go as often as we could. He was Sicilian, which has a different dialect of Italian than most areas. Mostly slang. My grandparents (on my father's side) were also from Sicily and used these types of slang words. I wanted to find out what some of them meant, and even if they were real words, but nobody was able to translate them.

One of the words was "bida doo". I knew what it meant (at least I thought I did) but wanted to find out if it really was a word that a Sicilian would know.

One night, we were walking into the La Louisiana restaurant and Franco was there.

"Franco," I said, "I have a question."

"What, Ricky?" he replied.

"What does 'bida doo' mean?"

"It's a far-tay, Ricky."

That's what *I* thought it meant!

Famous People Who Have Visited Gambino's

I'll let the pictures speak for themselves.

Goober (George
Lindsey) from Andy
Griffith Show

Yakov Smirnoff with Gari and Rick

George Kennedy

Gary Collins and Rick

Earnest Borgnine and
Art Carney

With Rick

Mickey Gilley

My friends Jenni and Fritz's house on Harson's Island

Dinner Theater Returns
With *Charlie's Aunt*

MARK JOHNSON
Staff Writer

Dinner theater returned to Fairhope last week as the Earth Drama Club teamed with Gambino's Restaurant to present a polished version of Charlie's Aunt.

The play is a typically English comedy complete with all the nuances and subtleties which characterize "English humor", and the Earth Drama cast carried it off...well..."smashingly" would probably be the best word.

Rick Gambino played the happy-golucky Lord Fancourt Babberly who pays a visit to a chum's Oxford rooms hoping to raid the liquor supply.

Instead, he finds Jack Chesney and Charles Wykeham (Wyly Gammon and Steve Crim) scheming to lure their True Loves to the room on the thin pretext of meeting Charlie's long-lost aunt from Brazil, a millionairess to be sure, but no doubt a tedious old crone with a face that would stop a clock.

For a time Jack and Charlie try to cajole "Babs" into being the old woman's escort while the two young bachelors make their proposals of marriage.

At the last minute, however, the rich aunt cables that she cannot make her schedule; instead of being Charlie's Aunt's escort, Babs must himself become Charlie's aunt. With a wig, a dress, a shawl and the best act he can muster, Babs becomes the keystone of the rest of the play's structure.

He is adored by the two young sweethearts (played by Cindy Powell and Ashley Atkins). They love to cuddle up to the old dowager and show their affection for such a sweet, harmless aunt ... and Babs is only to happy to return the compliment, thus infuriating Jack and Charlie.

Charlie's "aunt" is also courted by Jack's father, Sir Francis Chesney (played by Tut Wynne) and Stephen Spettigue (played by Guy Garner). Old Spettigue is the greedy gold-digger charged with the responsibility for protecting his niece and his ward who, naturally, are the two young ladies which Jack and Charlie wish to win away.

Just as things are starting to even out who should show up but the real a Donna Lucia D'Alvadorez (Played Brenda Henderson) and her adopted wa Ela Delahay (played by Melissa Whitter. The real aunt is surprised to learn that sh has already arrived, particularly when s finds "herself" indulging in such pursu as cigar-smoking.

From there, the confusion circuit overload, and the whole ploy come crashing down on its perpetrators. But that fall comes the final resolution a only abrasive old Spettigue is left hold the bag.

The only one who stays abreast confusion throughout is Brass Butler (Played by William Gl pilfers the champagne, tips him endures the cranky mating ca. Spettigue whose bark is worse bite.

The play was considerably di. than past material the club has tac Under the directorship of Gretchen Ri, the wealth of newcomers to the st. turned in highly commendable pe formances.

Worthy of special note was Rick Gambino's portrayal of Babs and his role-within-a-role performance as the bogus aunt. Gambino's sense of timing no doubt drew on a foundation of innate talent, but it also reflected the many hours of work which the director and th other actors spent polishing the action every movement, every transition every Victorian exchange of words. Ar e can put on a dowanger's dress look ludicrous for a few moments, t takes talent, support, good directic 'rd work to pile one level of r. ano another in the traditional e comedy".

Charlie's Aur' was ambitious theater t dialogue, ly intric clockwork talent the display.

'And What Am I To Do With *These?*'

Rick Gambino (r.) as "Charlie's Aunt" displays a bit of resistance as Jack Chesney (played by Wyly Gammon) attempts to persuade his friend to play along with the game. Earth Drama and Gambino's Restaurant teamed up last week to bring dinner theater back to the Eastern Shore.
(Courier Photo by Mark Johnson)

279

A duet at the piano with Art Carney and Rick

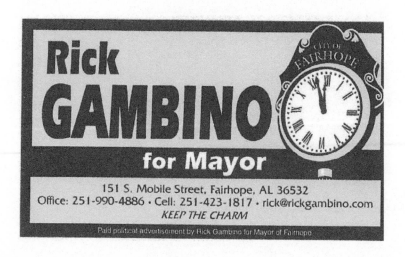

THE CAST

Lord Fancourt Babberly . . . . Rick Gambino
Jack Chesney . . . . Wyly Gammon
Charles Wykeham . . . . Steve Crim
Col. Sir Francis Chesney . . . . Tut Wynne
Stephen Spettigue . . . . Guy Garner
Brassett . . . . William Glass
Donna Lucia D'Alvadorez . . . . Brenda Hendersoi
Kitty Verdun . . . . Cindy Powell
Amy Spettigue . . . . Ashley Atkins
Ela Delahay . . . . Melissa Whitten

* * * *

Lord Fancourt (Babbs): "Hello! I'm Charlie's Aunt
from Brazil. . . where the nuts come from!"

Jack Chesney: "Charlie, do you know what a pious
fraud is?"

Charles Wykeham: "Stay where you are, do what you
like, only GET RID of him!"

Stephen Spettigue: "DARLING!"

Brasset: "Well, college gents will do anything. . ."

Donna Lucia: "Do I understand you to say that the Donna
Lucia D'Alvadorez is actually here?"

Kitty Verdun: "No. I must have his consent in writing."

Amy Spettigue: "Mr. Wykeham, I'll never forgive you!"

Ela Delahay: "That voice! It is. . . It is. . . Oh Nooooo!"

Playbill for Charlies Aunt

Andy used to come in to Ricks Place and
try out new comedy routines

Rick and friends

Never Give Up

Part Eight

The Rock of the Family

Gari Gambino

I haven't talked about Gari as much as I wanted to earlier, because I planned this separate section to write about her. As I mentioned in Part One, I met her when she was driving her dad's truck and she stopped at a stop light.

Gari was born in West Virginia in 1940. She had a sister and brother from both of her parents. They divorced and each married again. She has half-brothers from both parents. Her family moved to the Detroit area before she was a teenager. I met her when she was sixteen. She was a real looker. But it was her energy. Something about her that just grabbed me.

Gari and Mother

The Rock

Gari indeed was the rock of the family. It is amazing how she showed her love; not by words, but by her actions. She also may be the most giving person I have ever met. Which made me a lucky man. She found so much joy in her unselfishness. I do not think we could have achieved what we did without the large part she played throughout our relationship.

She would also tell you what she thought. Without reserve. Our employees feared her and respected her. She would return the same love and respect. Don't get me wrong. When they screwed up, they were on the receiving end of her wrath. But then she was over it.

I don't know anybody who loved their children more than Gari. It was like they never did anything wrong. She looked at problems with them just like they were a bump in the road. She always saw the good in them.

A Serious Conversation

One night after dinner, Gari and I were sitting at the dining room table and she showed me her hand.

"Look at my thumb, Rick."

It was twitching. She was unable to stop it.

"Well," I said, "let's go to the doctor and see what it is."

A few weeks later, she got the results of the tests. She came home, sat me down and said she had Parkinson's, but was relieved it was not something worse. This was in 2004.

Her disease progressed to the point we had to take her car keys away. She was livid about not being able to drive. Then dementia was added to her problems. She would not accept that diagnosis. She kept saying "The report said no dementia." So, I just didn't bring the subject up again.

Thirteen years later, she was at that same table with me, in a mental fog. She was thinking about something; I could see the worry in her eyes. She finally looked up at me, sitting in her wheelchair, and said, "You mean, I am not going to get better?"

That tore my heart out.

What could I say? I didn't want to lie. Her shoulders slumped a little, and I could see the hope drain out of her.

Inseparable

For years I took care of Gari, alone at first, until she started showing more signs of the disease. We hired a part-time caretaker for the times I could not be with her. I realized how

loyal and supportive she had been all of our lives, and also that our time together was coming to a close. I especially remember the moments we shared going out to have dinners together. Romantic. And sad. My thinking was to never put her in a nursing home.

As the end came closer, she looked at me and smiled. I suspect she wanted to let me know she would be okay. She didn't seem afraid to die, only sad about it. And finally, she gave up telling me she could drive. I knew that was dangerous for her as well as others.

Gari's Final Day

We all knew it was time. All my sons were there. Serena, too.

Gari could not talk. Her breathing was labored and difficult. Hospice was there, helping. They told us that even though she can't talk, she can hear you. Tell her to wiggle her toes to let you know she can hear you. When our sons talked, her toes wiggled. "Mom, we love you," that kind of thing.

The kids left. It was just me at the house on Mobile with a

hospice helper. I kissed Gari goodnight on her forehead, told her I loved her, and then went to bed in the next room. She died in the middle of the night. The caregiver came in and said she was gone. I went in by myself and I knew she was gone. I remember she looked peaceful. I kissed her on the forehead and told her I loved her. And I did.

I decided to have a memorial at Gambino's. Nicole, Brett's wife, put together a slide show to show on the TVs in the restaurant. It was wonderful, touching. We all got up and said something about her. The place was packed with hundreds of friends and acquaintances.

When I gave my talk, I got choked up and apologized for being unable to speak. I somehow got through it. I really missed Gari. It was a sad day.

She was always there for me, and supported every decision I made, whether she thought it was good or not. It is not often you can find someone who loves you that much, and I was lucky to have found her.

I was fortunate to experience her love for me, which was absolutely unconditional. She is very much missed.

(You can go to the website to see the slide show.)

Gari and Rick

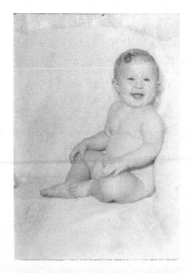

Gari as a baby

Jackie, Jimmy and Gari,
her brother and sister

Gari with sister, brother and
Dad

Gari in the service

Gari's sister Jackie

Gari and Rick

Gari as child, in the Navy
and smiling

Gambino Family

The happy couple

The Pebbles

Upper Row: Lucas Adam and Josh – Kneeling: Richard and Brett

Our Wonderful Sons

Richard:

Rich, my oldest son, is owner and operator of Pizzeria Delphina in Mobile Alabama. He has two children.

Brett:

Brett is the top sales rep for a major food distribution company. He is a talented musician and built and owns a state-of-the-art recording facility. He lives in Fairhope, Alabama, is married to Nicole, and has four children – two boys and two girls.

Adam:

Adam is a sales rep for a restaurant equipment company in Mobile, Alabama. He is married and has three children.

Josh:

Josh is general manager of two restaurants – Gambinos and the Pier Bar and Grill in Fairhope, Alabama. He is married and has four children

Lucas:

Lucas is an attorney and vice-president and general counsel for Coca Cola in the southeast. He lives in Birmingham, is married and has three children.

Never Give Up

Part Nine

What's in a Name?

'Ricardo' Gambino

The Gambino name has always been a point of contention with the public. I know most people wonder "Is he a part of the family or not?"

Throughout my life I've had both good and not-so-good experiences because of the name. I thought I would share a few of them with you here.

San Francisco

After a couple of years with Gambino's restaurant operating successfully, I felt it was time to take a real vacation, and we picked the Golden Gate city. I took Luke and his wife and we had a great time, with two incidents standing out during that trip.

We asked the hotel staff where we were staying downtown where we could get some good Italian food in Little Italy (yes, we love eating at other establishments and tasting the competition). They suggested a little place just right down the street.

It was a beautiful evening, so we walked to it and quickly found that others had heard of this restaurant, too – there was a line that went for half a block waiting to get in. A man in line said you had to go to the front of the line, put your name on the list and then get back in line. I went to do that.

"Can I a helpa you?" the older Italian gentleman asked.

"I was told to check in here."

"Whata your name is?" he asked

I said, "Gambino." I added a little Italian emphasis.

He stared for a second, thinking.

"Lemme a see your driver's license."

I thought that a strange request, but pulled it out and showed him. He smiled, nodded. Motioning with the fingers of his hand, he said, "Come on."

He sat us down. They brought out free antipasto and a full meal. It was delicious. We were pampered the whole time. I thanked him personally and he graciously smiled and said, "It's a nice a to meeta you."

When we left, I felt like I could slap everybody that was waiting in line.

Another time, we were walking around the city and found ourselves where the buses congregate and the drivers rested between runs. I walked up to a driver seated in the bus and asked him a couple of questions about where to go. He smiled, answered my questions and then asked how we were enjoying our trip.

"We're having a great time," I replied.

"Where you from?"

"Lincoln Park, originally."

"I have some old friends there," he said. "What's your name?"

"Rick Gambino."

I could see his whole demeanor change. For the better?

"Gambino?" he said. "Let me tell you something. Trust me. When your family took care of this bus line, it ran perfectly – better than any government agency has ever since."

At that time, Carlo Gambino's crime family was running a lot of San Francisco. He wiped his brow with a handkerchief.

"And they really took care of us," he continued. "A very smooth and efficient operation. I love them. So nice to meet you."

I didn't have the heart to tell him I was not one of those Gambinos, but he looked so happy I didn't want to bust his Zen moment. But we were distant relatives to those Gambinos, so I felt like the fellow didn't waste his time. If I ever ran into one of the Gambino goombas, I would pass it on. So far, it has never happened.

I thanked him and moved on.

Loan Shark?

My sons were out front one day at my house on Mobile Street. I had already purchased it from my dad. They were doing something out in the yard and these two older guys walk right past them and right up to the front door.

My kids turned around and wondered if these were Jehovah Witnesses or what?

They knocked on the door and I answered. "Can I help you guys with something?"

They said, "No, we're here to see Mr. Gambino."

I tell them "Well, I'm Mr. Gambino."

They said, "No, we're here to see the older Mr. Gambino."

"He doesn't live here anymore," I told them. "Can I help you with something?"

"Well, maybe."

They proceeded to ask if they could get a loan. They said they would pay a high interest and that they were good for it.

I told them I didn't do that, and I didn't know anybody who did. Maybe they could go to a bank or something.

They left pretty quickly.

They just assumed, I guess, Gambino—he's a loan shark; let's go to him and get money.

Wrong Question...

There were three guys coming into the restaurant, returning about three or four times. They told me they were called the Brooklyn Boys, but shared with me as an aside that Joey T. was Carlo Gambino's righthand man back in the day.

Brooklyn Boys with Rick at Gambino's. Joey T third from left

I always felt they were trying to recruit me, although they never came right out and said so.

I met them in the lobby one of the times they were at the restaurant. I was joking around with them, making small chit chat, when I asked Joey what did the T stand for. His demeaner changed, he looked at me and said, "None of your f**king business." That shut me up real quick.

To this day I don't know what the T stands for, and quite frankly, don't care. They continued coming in and we were friendly, but I stopped asking questions and we got along fine.

One of the Brooklyn Boys, Tony S., called me late one night after they had left the restaurant. I was asleep in bed. "Hey, Rick," he said, "I got pulled over in Daphne. You need to get me out of here." I guessed he was picked up for DUI.

I told him that I didn't have any more pull than he did with the police. If I could help, I sure would, but there was nothing I could do that would help him.

He wasn't happy and hung up. That was the last I saw of any of them.

Basketball

My sons played basketball and I coached them. One of the problems with going to your kids' games, especially if you are a coach, is you tend to want to overcompensate for them. This extends to the referee's calls.

Once, a referee called a penalty on my son that I felt was totally unjustified. I was very animated as a coach. I ran up to him on the sidelines and let him know. He shouted back at me and we got into a verbal fight. Of course, I had no chance of winning. He was the ref. But I let him know how I felt.

We ended up winning the game but losing the finals in overtime.

Later that night, I received a call from this ref.

"Mr. Gambino," he said.

"Yes?"

"Mr. Gambino, this is ____, the referee at the game today."

"Yeah, can I help you?"

"I … I just wanted to apologize for my yelling today and hope you didn't take it too seriously. I was out of line and realize it now."

I thought for a moment and realized why he called. "It's no problem, I was out of line, too. Let's just forget it."

"That's great. Thank you so much, Mr. Gambino."

He hung up and I smiled. He probably thought I was going to initiate a hit on him or something. I found out later that some of my sons' friends went to him and explained who they thought I was.

With the name Gambino, it was another case of mistaken identity.

EASTERN SHORE COURIER, Wednesday, March 4, 1987 Page 7A

Gold

Rick Gambino's Gold team is the Advanced division winner in the Eastern Shore Youth Basketball Association. Team members from left are, back row, Assistant Coach Adam Gambino, Kenneth Hoffren, Will Shaffer, Coach Rick Gambino, front row, Josh Gambino, Luke Gambino and Scott Myrick. Not pictured is Ajex Cantrall.

Wise Guys

I have been accused of being in the Gambino crime family most of my life. Not overtly, but subtly, as I have shared in this book. Doesn't matter that it is not true. Innuendo is all it takes. As I've shown you in this book, sometimes it is to my advantage, and sometimes not.

I did have an idea I knew would be controversial.

Part of the strategy for Gambino's has been to offer entertainment in addition to great food. I've mentioned the different shows we've done, and I played for many years in the bar lounge. We decided to hire a piano player I'd known about for years named Scott. Part of the package was to create a unique atmosphere for him in the lounge area.

The theme picked was ... a piano. We painted the bar counter, put a bar around the piano and a mirror above the

keyboard so people could see him playing. He is a fantastic entertainer, and the crowds confirmed it. The bar tops we painted like piano keys by my cousin Sam Gambino.

That's when we came up with the name Wiseguys Lounge. I also decided to have a little fun and turn my lounge into a mafia museum with pictures of the heads of the New York crime families – including my second cousin Carlo Gambino.

I know many people think it may be true (that I am connected to the family somehow), but certainly the majority realize it is tongue-in-cheek and a nod to the family name.

By the way, my son Luke recently took a trip to Italy and Sicily and met some of our relatives. They confirmed my grandfather's relationship to Carlo Gambino.

Turns out all the Gambinos are related by blood.

Our salad dressing

Paula Deen, Rick and Nicole (Brett's wife)

Never Give Up

Part Ten

Closing Thoughts

Gambino Family

As I look back on my childhood, I see a very confused kid. As I've mentioned, my parents divorced when I was eight and I can't really blame anybody for it, because they were great parents.

Things were hard for my mom, as she was working and raising three kids. We didn't have a car, TV or any of the other so-called luxuries until much later on in my childhood. However, I never felt deprived because everybody else where we lived was in the same boat or worse. I think I had my career so much on my mind I didn't think on much else.

I really didn't understand the moral concept of right and wrong. If I wanted to do it, that's all that mattered. But I was never the kind of person who wanted to hurt others. I'm not saying this as an excuse. It is simply the way it was with me.

Because I was selfish, I didn't think beyond what I was doing to realize it might hurt someone else. When I took someone's car for a joyride, I didn't look at the damage I might be doing to that person. I guess that, as an adolescent (or should I say delinquent), I was far too self-focused, and I'm certainly not proud of that.

However, I'm so thankful that before I got out of my teens, I realized that what I'd done for fun had a negative impact on other people's lives.

I wish I could go back to everyone whom I hurt and personally apologize to them.

Since I can't, I'm apologizing now.

My Familia

I loved my family always. The only thing I regret is not telling them enough and not showing them my feelings and

The Gambino stairsteps

sincere love for them. I also am sorry about how my lack of expressing those feelings may have had an effect on them. I wish I could change all of that.

It is so sad that it takes so many years to realize what you should have done, and then you wish that you could go back and do things differently. There is no doubt about the love that exists in our family. However, I could probably count on two hands the number of times my wife Gari and I actually said, "I love you".

But there is no doubt that love is what held us, and the family, together for fifty-four years and counting.

And, so far, I have ended up with seventeen grandchildren, and three great grandchildren.

Thankfully, we have a God who understands and knows what's inside each person's heart.

Music

A theme running through this book is my lifelong love for music. As you already know, music played an important part in my life. In fact, in many respects I thought it was the most important part of my life … until the offer to play in Las Vegas was made. That was a turning point for me, a sort of growing up. I felt the temptation but it meant I would have to leave my family for a while. Also, I had just made a serious commitment to my Christian life and I felt compelled to pursue it. I had to make a difficult life choice.

Maybe choosing Las Vegas would have been the stepping-stone to a much bigger and better career. However, even though I wasn't always a believer and, at times, had some doubts, I had always had a personal relationship with God. I was excited about totally surrendering my life to Him and following Him all the way. I had to find out what a real commitment to God would do in my life. So, I made the choice.

That being said, I was planning on getting out of the nightclubs because I didn't think it was a good environment to sustain a dedicated Christian life, and it would be a strain on my family. A grown-up decision that I have never regretted.

There is another thread weaving its way through my tale and it is my love for my family.

My Health

God has blessed me with fairly good health. I've done things to screw that up with some unnecessary surgeries because of my determination for perfection, which I catered to over my health and wellbeing. The things I had done surgically mostly turned out to make things worse. Especially for my singing. That ability is no longer an option.

313

Fortunately, my relations on both sides lived into their 80s and 90s, including my aunt Marion on my mother's side, who recently died at 104. I only have one aunt and uncle left: Uncle Richard, 87, and Aunt Mildred, 94, and both seem to be in good health. On my dad's side, the oldest was Uncle Joe, who recently died at 98.

The interesting thing about my uncles and aunts on both sides is that on my mother's side there were six girls and two boys, and on my father's side there were six boys and two girls. Wouldn't those have been interesting marriages?

Think and Grow Rich... really?

I remember when we first moved to Fairhope, I read an interesting book called *Think and Grow Rich* by Napoleon Hill. It made a huge impression on me. In it napoleon Hill said it was important to write down the actual money you wanted to make and have a target date in mind you wanted it by.

I took this to heart and wrote the letter the book said I was to write. It included 'by this date' I want to make a certain amount of money'. I wrote down the date I wanted and the amount of $75,000.

Turned out by that date I had exceeded that amount and realized that trying hard and setting goals was going to be critical in my future life. Like they say, the un-aimed arrow always hits its target. I made sure my future arrows always had an exact target to hit.

Give Up? Never...

Giving up was never an option for me. When times were uncertain (and there were plenty), there was something inside of me that helped me look past the uncertainty. At times, I didn't know where life was leading me, but my drive to keep going was intense.

My goal was always to be the best in whatever I did. Only a few can achieve that. But if you set that as your goal, you can accomplish much. I loved everything I did, whether it was music, singing or the restaurant business.

Going to work every day was not a struggle. I was always totally motivated. A lot of my time lying in bed was spent thinking of ideas to make whatever I was working on better.

We currently have weekly meetings at my restaurant with the idea of sharing with the employees that exact idea. To do better and improve. I guess the meetings I had as a young musician with the group stuck with me.

I would share the following with my employees:

- Set your targets high.
- Never be satisfied with mediocrity.
- Do your homework and learn from the best.
- If you do miss the target, you'll at least come close..
- Make sure there is a market for your dream
- And continue trying.

I have found that if you really please yourself, without hurting others, you'll have a good chance of pleasing other people. I don't regret my failures, because I always learned from them. Fear of failure, which, thank God, I never had, is what holds so many people back from achieving their dreams and doing what they love to do.

I have observed many people with little talent and limited ability become very successful; mainly because they never give up. They get back up one more time.

On the other hand, there's the person who is extremely gifted and can do just about anything he attempts, but he remains confined in his own little world. Mediocre. He doesn't have the resolve and, based on fear of failure, remains stuck with something that makes him unhappy.

It makes you wonder if what we normally call success is really success, and what is the ultimate road to true happiness and fulfillment.

My Philosophy

I guess it was my absence of fear that was the driving force of whatever success I have attained. My thoughts were really *what did I have to lose*? I never really remember saying that to myself, but deep down in my subconscious it was there. My vision was never obstructed with the fear of failure,

I had so many friends, strangers and even family tell me at times not to do something. I basically said to myself, *Why not*? I think many of the people who "advised me" in that way didn't advance very far in life for one simple reason: they failed to look beyond that day to see what the future could bring if they dared to try.

I truly loved the journey I took to make a future for myself and my family. Don't get me wrong. I did experience occasional normal fear, just not when it came to my endeavors.

I feel that if a person honestly looked at what they love and what they would love to do, and did it, they would be successful at it, rather than just doing something that might become available to them. Desire it and don't take your eye off of it. That seems to be the key.

The best gift in business is common sense, and yet it is usually in short supply. You can't go to school to learn it. You need to trust yourself. With some exceptions, the stuff you learn at school, for the most part, is good for conversations at parties. The real business of life takes more. A lot more.

I run my restaurants from the customer's chair. Way too many owners run it from the office, crunching numbers, forgetting who actually pays the bills. That's where common sense comes in. By putting yourself in the customer's place, you can use your common sense to see what they need. And satisfying customers has been the foundation of all the successes I've had in the restaurant business.

One other tidbit: Be better than your competitors. Be sure you know what they are doing, and then beat them at their game. Do it better.

I also think that hard work is more, or at least as important, as talent, because while you are working, you're experiencing what does and does not work. Making mistakes is an education you don't have to pay for – except with your time. Of course, if you combine that with talent, you have the best of both worlds.

My endeavors in the restaurant business turned work into personal motivation, so I never really saw it as work. I also feel that Gari was right there with the same attitude. What a blessing I had.

Most people that I know who are successful, got there by hard work. I do know some who had their fortune dropped in their lap. They were in the minority, and many of them ended up losing that fortune, with an exceptional few who took the ball and ran with it.

In all these cases, I have found that it is up to each one of us to make our own path, and we are each responsible for what we achieve.

Closing Thoughts

Before I sign off, I want to leave you with these closing thoughts.

Being rich was never my goal. Being famous was never my goal. Being the best, in whatever I did, however, was the driving force behind everything I did in life

Having said that, I know now what is, and has always been, important to me: God, family and friends. With these three, I am tremendously blessed.

And happy.

Because of this, I feel that my life story, with all its twists and turns, is worth sharing with those who care about me.

There is value to be found in my life's experiences, both the foolish ones and the ones that turned out to be wise.

Doing what I love

October 1975

"By the first day of January, 1981, I will have in my possession $75,000.00 which will come to me in various amounts from time to time during the interim. In return for the money I will give the most efficient service in which I am capable, rendering the fullest possible quantity, and the best possible quality of service in the capacity of restaurant owner. I believe I will have this money in my possession. My faith is so strong I can now see this money before my eyes. I can touch it with my hands. It is now awaiting transfer to me at the time, and in the proportion that I deliver the service I intend to render in return for it. I am awaiting a plan by which to accumulate this money. And I will follow that plan, when it is received."

The letter I wrote for Think and Grow Rich

Mark, my brother, and his wife Barb

My sister Serena with Dad and Beulah

Smiling Rick

Rick, his Dad, and Rick's
five sons

Luke, my son

Many of the videos mentioned in this book are available to view at: **www.NeverGiveUpBook.com**

Additionally, there are way too many pictures to put in the book, and they are available on the website as well.

Thanks to Sam Gambino
for the cover artwork

Sam with his family

www.SamGambino.com

Made in the USA
Monee, IL
26 September 2023

43504641R00198